ACTS

(chapters 1–14)
The Church Catches Fire

D1450545

PROJECT DIRECTOR:

James F. Couch, Jr.

WRITING & EDITORIAL TEAM:

Keith Madsen, Cathy Tardif, Katy Harris

PRODUCTION TEAM:

Sharon Penington, Erika Tiepel

SERENDIPITY HOUSE • LITTLETON, COLORADO

Published by Serendipity House Publisher
Littleton, Colorado

International Standard Book Number: 1-57494-092-9

07 08 09 10 11 / 10 9 8 7 6 5

ACKNOWLEDGMENTS

To Zondervan Bible Publishers
for permission to use
the NIV text,
The Holy Bible, New International Bible Society.
© 1973, 1978, 1984 by International Bible Society.
Used by permission of Zondervan Bible Publishers.

Serendipity House
8100 South Park Way, A-6
Littleton, CO 80120
1-800-525-9563 / www.serendipityhouse.com

TABLE OF CONTENTS

CORE VALUES

Community: The purpose of this curriculum is to build community within the body of believers around Jesus Christ.

Group Process: To build community, the curriculum must be designed to take a group through a step-by-step process of sharing your story with one another.

Interactive Bible Study: To share your "story," the approach to Scripture in the curriculum needs to be open-ended and right brain—to "level the playing field" and encourage everyone to share.

Developmental Stages: To provide a healthy program throughout the four stages of the life cycle of a group, the curriculum needs to offer courses on three levels of commitment: (1) Beginner Level— low-level entry, high structure, to level the playing field; (2) Growth Level—deeper Bible study, flexible structure, to encourage group accountability; (3) Discipleship Level—in-depth Bible study, open structure, to move the group into high gear.

Target Audiences: To build community throughout the culture of the church, the curriculum needs to be flexible, adaptable and transferable into the structure of the average church.

INTRODUCTION

Each healthy small group will move through various stages as it matures.

Growth Stage: Here the group begins to care for one another as it learns to apply what they learn through Bible study, worship and prayer.

Develop Stage: The inductive Bible study deepens while the group members discover and develop gifts and skills. The group explores ways to invite their neighbors and coworkers to group meetings.

Birth Stage: This is the time in which group members form relationships and begin to develop community. The group will spend more time in ice-breaker exercises, relational Bible study and covenant building.

Multiply Stage: The group begins the multiplication process. Members pray about their involvement in new groups. The "new" groups begin the lifecycle again with the Birth Stage.

Subgrouping: If you have nine or more people at a meeting, Serendipity recommends you divide into subgroups of 3–6 for the Bible study. Ask one person to be the leader of each subgroup and to follow the directions for the Bible study. After 30 minutes, the Group Leader will call "time" and ask all subgroups to come together for the Caring Time.

Each group meeting should include all parts of the "three-part agenda."

 Ice-Breaker: Fun, history-giving questions are designed to warm the group and to build understanding about the other group members. You can choose to use all of the Ice-Breaker questions, especially if there is a new group member that will need help in feeling comfortable with the group.

 Bible Study: The heart of each meeting is the reading and examination of the Bible. The questions are open, discover questions that lead to further inquiry. Reference notes are provided to give everyone a "level playing field." The emphasis is on understanding what the Bible says and applying the truth to real life. The questions for each session build. There is always at least one "going deeper" question provided. You should always leave time for the last of the "questions for interaction." Should you choose, you can use the optional "going deeper" question to satisfy the desire for the challenging questions in groups that have been together for a while.

 Caring Time: All study should point us to actions. Each session ends with prayer and direction in caring for the needs of the group members. You can choose between several questions. You should always pray for the "empty chair." Who do you know that could fill that void in your group?

Sharing Your Story: These sessions are designed for members to share a little of their personal lives each time. Through a number of special techniques each member is encouraged to move from low risk less personal sharing to higher risk responses. This helps develop the sense of community and facilitates care giving.

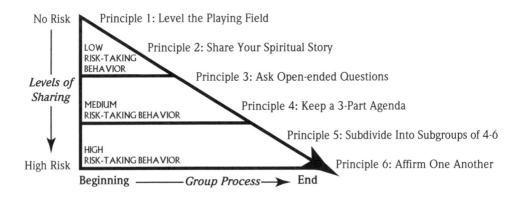

Group Covenant: A group covenant is a "contract" that spells out your expectations and the ground rules for your group. It's very important that your group discuss these issues—preferably as part of the first session.

GROUND RULES:

- *Priority:* While you are in the group, you give the group meeting priority.

- *Participation:* Everyone participates and no one dominates.

- *Respect:* Everyone is given the right to their own opinion and all questions are encouraged and respected.

- *Confidentiality:* Anything that is said in the meeting is never repeated outside the meeting.

- *Empty Chair.* The group stays open to new people at every meeting.

- *Support:* Permission is given to call upon each other in time of need—even in the middle of the night.

- *Advice Giving:* Unsolicited advice is not allowed.

- *Mission:* We agree to do everything in our power to start a new group as our mission.

ISSUES:

- The time and place this group is going to meet is:_____

- Responsibility for refreshments is: _____

- Childcare is _____ responsibility.

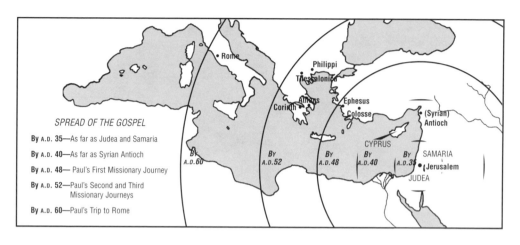

SPREAD OF THE GOSPEL

By A.D. 35—As far as Judea and Samaria

By A.D. 40—As far as Syrian Antioch

By A.D. 48— Paul's First Missionary Journey

By A.D. 52—Paul's Second and Third
Missionary Journeys

By A.D. 60—Paul's Trip to Rome

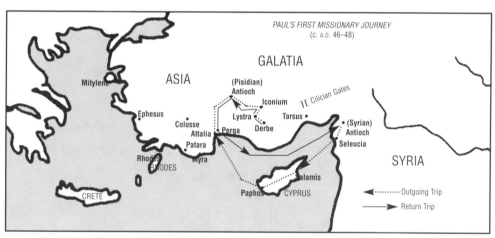

PAUL'S FIRST MISSIONARY JOURNEY
(C. A.D. 46–48)

GALATIA

ASIA

Mitylene

(Pisidian) Antioch
Iconium
Lystra
Derbe
Tarsus
Cilician Gates

Ephesus
Colosse
Attalia
Patara
Perga
Myra
Rhodes
RHODES

(Syrian) Antioch
Seleucia

SYRIA

CRETE

Salamis
Paphos
CYPRUS

Outgoing Trip
Return Trip

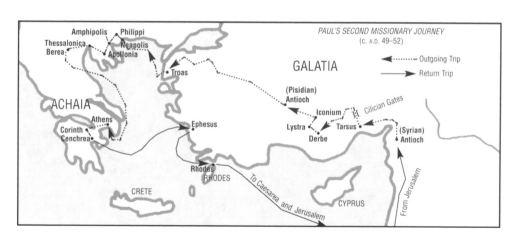

PAUL'S SECOND MISSIONARY JOURNEY
(C. A.D. 49–52)

Outgoing Trip
Return Trip

Amphipolis Philippi
Thessalonica Neapolis
Berea Apollonia
Troas

GALATIA

(Pisidian) Antioch
Iconium
Cilician Gates
Lystra Tarsus
Derbe
(Syrian) Antioch

ACHAIA

Athens
Corinth
Cenchrea

Ephesus

Rhodes
RHODES

To Caesarea and Jerusalem
From Jerusalem

CRETE

CYPRUS

Session 1
Jesus Ascends To Heaven
Scripture   Acts 1:1–11

WELCOME

Welcome to this study of Acts! Together we will find inspiration and encouragement as we learn about the coming of the Holy Spirit, the birth of the church and the exciting growth of Christianity.

Although Luke is nowhere named within Acts as author, there is a strong and ancient tradition that he did, indeed, write this book as a companion piece to the third Gospel. He is mentioned only three times in the New Testament (Col. 4:14; 2 Tim. 4:11; Philem. 24). From these references, it can be deduced that Luke was a physician, a valued companion of Paul and a Gentile. Luke's role as Paul's traveling companion is evident in the book of Acts. In the four so-called *we* sections, the author suddenly switches from saying, "They did this" to "We did that" (16:10–17; 20:5–21:18; 27:1–28:16). We learn that Luke was a Gentile from the list of greetings with which Paul concludes Colossians. In Colossians 4:12, Paul begins a set of greetings presumably from the Gentiles in the party. Luke's name is included in this latter list.

The date of the final events recorded here took place in early A.D. 60, so Acts must have been completed after that time.

The theme of the book of Acts is to spread the Gospel to all the known world (1:8).

Why did Luke write the book of Acts? One reason must have been his desire to commend Christianity to the Gentile world in general and to the Roman government in particular. The Good News about Jesus is not just for Jews but for all people. Not surprisingly, therefore, we find in Acts not only Jews turning to Jesus (3,000 on the day of Pentecost, see 2:41), but also Gentiles. We see Philip preaching to the Samaritans and Jewish believers and evangelizing Gentiles in Antioch. In particular, we find Paul called by Christ to be the apostle to the Gentiles, setting up churches across the Roman Empire. Finally in Acts 15, there is formal affirmation that Gentiles are accepted in the church of Jesus Christ on equal terms with Jews. Luke seemed to go out of his way to show that followers of Christ were loyal citizens and not lawbreakers and criminals (18:14–16; 19:37; 23:29; 25:25). He also took pains to point out that Roman officials had always treated followers of Christ fairly and courteously (18:12–17; 19:31). This was important to state lest Christianity be perceived as a political movement and therefore a threat to the Roman Empire. However, commending Christianity to the Gentiles was probably not Luke's central aim. His main purpose is implicit in 1:8, "But you will receive power when the Holy Spirit comes on you; and you will be my witnesses in Jerusalem, and in all Judea and Samaria, and to the ends of the earth. Luke's aim was to show how, in 30 short years, Christianity had spread from Jerusalem to Rome.

The book of Acts is the bridge between the Gospels (Matthew, Mark, Luke and John) and the Epistles. Acts continues the story of Jesus. It shows how his life, death and resurrection brought a whole new community into existence: the church. On the other hand, Acts sets the stage for the correspondence to this church; the letters make up the rest of the New Testament. At many points it would be difficult to get the full sense of what the Epistles are saying without the data found in Acts. Luke tells the story of the development of the church by opening a series of windows that allows us to glimpse important developments in its growth.

ICE-BREAKER   15 Min.
CONNECT WITH YOUR GROUP

LEADER

Be sure to read the introductory material in the front of this book prior to this first session. To help your group members get acquainted, have each person introduce him or herself and then take turns answering one or two of the Ice-Breaker questions. If time allows, you may want to discuss all three questions.

Today we are beginning a journey together by studying about a difficult good-bye! Take some time to get to know one another by sharing your responses to the following questions.

1. When have you experienced a very difficult time saying good-bye to someone?

2. When you have to say good-bye to someone, do you more typically drag it out, or try to make it as quick and painless as possible?

3. When you were an adolescent or younger adult, who did you consider to be your mentor? In what area of life did you learn the most from this person?

BIBLE STUDY   30 Min.
READ SCRIPTURE AND DISCUSS

LEADER

Ask four members of the group to read out loud Acts 1:1–11. Have one member read Luke's narration; another read the part of Jesus (vv. 7–8); the other two read the part of the angels (v. 11); and the whole group read the words of the disciples in verse 6. Then discuss the questions that follow. Be sure to save time at the end for the Caring Time.

In today's Scripture passage, we stand in awe with the disciples as Jesus miraculously ascends into heaven. Imagine what it must have been like for the disciples to say good-bye to their friend, mentor and Savior as you listen to Acts 1:1–11.

Jesus Ascends to Heaven

Luke: *In my former book, Theophilus, I wrote about all that Jesus began to do and to teach [2] until the day he was taken up to heaven, after giving instructions through the Holy Spirit to the apostles he had chosen. [3] After his suffering, he showed himself to these men and gave many convincing proofs that he was alive. He appeared to them over a period of forty days and spoke about the kingdom of God. [4] On one occasion, while he was eating with them, he gave them this command:*

Jesus: *"Do not leave Jerusalem, but wait for the gift my Father promised, which you have heard me speak about. [5] For John baptized with water, but in a few days you will be baptized with the Holy Spirit."*

Disciples:	*⁶So when they met together, they asked him, "Lord, are you at this time going to restore the kingdom to Israel?"*
Jesus:	*⁷He said to them: "It is not for you to know the times or dates the Father has set by his own authority. ⁸But you will receive power when the Holy Spirit comes on you; and you will be my witnesses in Jerusalem, and in all Judea and Samaria, and to the ends of the earth."*
Luke:	*⁹After he said this, he was taken up before their very eyes, and a cloud hid him from their sight. ¹⁰They were looking intently up into the sky as he was going, when suddenly two men dressed in white stood beside them.*
Angels:	*¹¹"Men of Galilee," they said, "why do you stand here looking into the sky? This same Jesus, who has been taken from you into heaven, will come back in the same way you have seen him go into heaven."*

Acts 1:1–11

LEADER

Be sure to read the Summary and Study Notes at the conclusion of this session and refer to these during the discussion time when needed. If 30 minutes is not enough time to answer all of the questions in this section, conclude the Bible Study by answering question #7.

QUESTIONS FOR INTERACTION

1. *If you had been*
~~Had you been~~ with Jesus when he was getting ready to return to heaven, what one last question would you have wanted to ask him?

2. What "convincing proofs" (v. 3) have you seen that Jesus Christ really is alive?

3. Why was it so important for Jesus to be with the disciples for this forty-day period?

4. Why was it important for the disciples to wait for the Holy Spirit?

5. Is it hard or easy for you to just wait? What makes it easy or hard for you?

6. In verse 8 Jesus says, "You will be my witnesses." Where do you feel most called to witness for Christ? Do you feel more passion for witnessing to those in your own town and country (Jerusalem and Judea), or to those in other countries ("to the ends of the earth")?

7. What do you think needs to be the next step in order for you to witness in the way this passage calls you to witness?
   ❐ Receiving the Holy Spirit in a way you have not already.
   ❐ Resolving to stop "staring into heaven" and being a spectator.
   ❐ Spending some time with Jesus in order to learn more.
   ❐ Other_____.

13

GOING DEEPER: *If your group has time and/or wants a challenge, go on to this question.*

8. How do you know when it is time to "wait for the Holy Spirit," and when you are ready to act? When do you know you have received all the guidance, power and direction you are going to get?

CARING TIME   15 Min.

APPLY THE LESSON AND PRAY FOR ONE ANOTHER

LEADER

Take some extra time in this first session to go over the introductory material at the beginning of this book. At the close, pass around your books and have everyone sign the Group Directory inside the front cover.

This very important time is for developing and expressing your concern for each other as group members by praying for one another.

1. Have your group agree on its group covenant and ground rules.

2. Begin the prayer time by taking turns and sharing the first name of a person with whom you would like to share the Good News of Jesus. Ask for the Holy Spirit to prepare that person's heart and give you the right words to say.

3. Pray specifically for God to lead you to someone to bring next week to fill the empty chair.

4. Share any other prayer requests and then close in prayer.

NEXT WEEK

Today we were reminded that we are called by Jesus to spread his message of salvation to people of every race and nation. At first glance this sounds like an impossible task, but we can be comforted by the fact that we are not alone in this endeavor. We have the Holy Spirit to help us. Resolve to spend a quiet time in prayer each day in the coming week and listen for the Holy Spirit's guidance. Next week we will learn more about the Holy Spirit and his role in our lives.

Notes on Acts 1:1–11

Summary: Acts is the book that tells what the first disciples did in response to God's revelation of himself in Jesus Christ. But ironically enough the book starts with the disciples not sure how—or whether—they should act at all. They knew that big changes were coming to their world, but they were unsure of their role in it all.

There are basically three different ways of looking at the human role and responsibility for changing the world. One is "God isn't going to do anything, so we have to do it all." We might call this the "Tower of Babel" philosophy (Gen. 11:1–9). People were worried about being scattered over the face of the earth, thereby losing some of the community and strength that comes through unity. So they acted on their own to build a "tower to heaven" that would serve as a visual rallying point and hold them together. It would also build their egos. With it they would "make a name for themselves" (Gen. 11:4). This philosophy of "we have to do it all ourselves" is what drives secular science. Science has done great things for human progress. But some look to it to "save" us—to deliver us from all of our problems, as the Tower of Babel was to do for that era. But science can just as quickly destroy us as save us. We need only look at the tremendous build-up of nuclear, chemical and biological weaponry to realize that.

The disciples who were around at the time had seen God raise Christ from the dead. They were not very tempted to believe the idea that "God isn't going to do anything so we have to do it all." Instead they had a second way of thinking that "God will do everything, so we don't have to do anything." Jesus had spent three years teaching and training them to take over. After it was all over, what do they do?—they stand around gazing at the heavens (vv. 10–11), waiting to see what Jesus was going to do next! They didn't seem to understand that "what happens next" was what *they* were supposed to do.

This leads to the third philosophy about the human role in relation to God and how God is changing the world: "God will act; and an important part of his action will be what he does through *us*." Jesus had tried to impress this approach on them all along (Mark 9:14–19; Luke 10:1–20; John 14:12). In this passage from John in particular Jesus makes the astonishing promise that his disciples will be able to do even greater things than he himself had done—if they act in his name. In reality, the book of Acts is the story of how Jesus began to fulfill that promise.

1:1 *my former book.* That is, the Gospel of Luke. Church tradition is unanimous in its witness that Luke authored both works. *Theophilus.* An unknown figure. *all that Jesus began to do and to teach.* This is a clue to the way one should view this book—it is the continuing story of the work of Jesus through his Spirit in the life of his body, the church.

1:2 *until the day he was taken up to heaven.* The Ascension does not mark the end of Jesus' ministry, but simply a new phase of his work. He now exercises his divine reign from heaven. *through the Holy Spirit.* The Spirit played an important part in the earthly ministry of Jesus (in his conception—Luke 1:35; his announcement—Luke 2:26; as a summary of his purpose—Luke 3:16; in his baptism—Luke 3:22; in his temptation—Luke 4:1; in his teaching—Luke 4:14; in his prayers—Luke 11:13; and in his expectation for the future—Luke 24:49). *apostles.* See Luke

6:12–16. Apostles were ambassadors especially commissioned to represent the one in whose name they were sent.

1:3 *the kingdom of God.* The announcement of the reign of God through which he saves his people was the theme of Jesus' earthly ministry as well (Luke 4:43).

1:4 *but wait ...* The disciples might have taken this to mean that they were just to wait around while God acted. In reality, God was telling them to wait until God empowered and directed them to act. This he was about to do through the sending of the Holy Spirit (Acts 2). While God wants us to act, sometimes it is appropriate to wait until God's power and direction comes. ***the gift my Father promised.*** This gift is the Holy Spirit (Isa. 32:15; Joel 2:28–32; Luke 11:13; 12:12; 24:49; Gal. 3:14). Jesus quotes the words of John the Baptist (Luke 3:16) as a reminder that from the beginning the expectation was that through him the Spirit of God would be poured out on all people. ***baptized with the Holy Spirit.*** Baptism was associated with cleansing. The metaphor would communicate a being flooded with God's Spirit.

1:8 This verse embraces the twin themes of the whole book. The mission of Jesus is continued through the work of his Spirit empowering and enabling the disciples to bear witness of him (Matt. 28:18–20; Luke 12:11–12). The result of this empowering will be the spread of the Gospel throughout the world—from the spiritual heart of Israel (Jerusalem) to the immediate vicinity (Judea) to the dispersed Samaritans in the adjacent province to the north, to the outermost reaches of the earth. The book of Acts is built around these geographical markers.

Chapters 1:1–6:7 occur in Jerusalem and Judea; 6:8–9:31 deals with events that lead the church to Samaria; and 9:32 on recounts the chain of events that leads Paul to journey throughout much of the Roman empire with the Good News of Jesus. Note that Jesus' answer is more inclusive than the disciples' question as far as the mission described. They talked of restoring Israel—he responded with a mission that would start in Jerusalem and then go to "the ends of the earth." He had come to bring spiritual freedom, freedom from sin, guilt and death, and to bring it to all people.

1:9 *a cloud hid him from their sight.* This is not a statement of weather conditions at the time, but a declaration of Jesus' deity. See also Daniel 7:13–14.

1:11 The Mount of Olives, where the Ascension occurred (v. 12), was just outside of the city. The angels' message picks up on Zechariah 14:4, which teaches that the Messiah will one day appear on that mountain when he comes to fully establish his reign. ***This same Jesus ... will come back.*** Here we are reminded of a teaching of Jesus recorded in Matthew 24:42–51. He said, "Therefore keep watch, because you do not know on what day your Lord will come." He then tells a parable to say what we should be doing: "Who then is the faithful and wise servant, whom the master has put in charge of his servants in his household to give them their food at the proper time? It will be good for that servant whose master finds him doing so when he returns." This indicates that we are not called to stand around passively waiting for Christ's return. We are called to be sharing the Gospel and acting in love toward the people around us.

THE DAY OF PENTECOST

SCRIPTURE   ACTS 2:1–13

LAST WEEK

Last week we studied how the disciples were told just before Jesus' ascension that the Holy Spirit would soon come upon them to empower them as witnesses. This week we will study the powerful way that promise was fulfilled.

ICE-BREAKER   15 Min.
CONNECT WITH YOUR GROUP

LEADER

Begin the session with a word of prayer. Have your group members take turns sharing their response to one, two or three of the Ice-Breaker questions. Be sure that everyone gets a chance to participate.

Every person has unique experiences to share. Get to know each other better by sharing some of those experiences.

1. When have you had an experience in a group that was so amazing and unique you had a hard time explaining it to people who weren't there?

2. With what other cultures did you have contact as a child or adolescent? Were the relationships between the cultures in your neighborhood or town relaxed or tense?

3. What adult do you remember who really "spoke your language" when you were an adolescent?

BIBLE STUDY

READ SCRIPTURE AND DISCUSS

30 Min.

LEADER

Have a member of the group, selected ahead of time, read aloud the passage from Acts. (Someone who doesn't mind trying difficult words!) Then discuss the questions that follow. Be sure to save time at the end for the Caring Time.

The promise Jesus made to his disciples about the coming of the Holy Spirit is fulfilled in today's Scripture passage. Listen to Acts 2:1–13 as we witness once again the power of the Holy Spirit and the birthday of the church.

The Holy Spirit Comes at Pentecost

2 When the day of Pentecost came, they were all together in one place. ²Suddenly a sound like the blowing of a violent wind came from heaven and filled the whole house where they were sitting. ³They saw what seemed to be tongues of fire that separated and came to rest on each of them. ⁴All of them were filled with the Holy Spirit and began to speak in other tongues as the Spirit enabled them.

⁵Now there were staying in Jerusalem God-fearing Jews from every nation under heaven. ⁶When they heard this sound, a crowd came together in bewilderment, because each one heard them speaking in his own language. ⁷Utterly amazed, they asked: "Are not all these men who are speaking Galileans? ⁸Then how is it that each of us hears them in his own native language? ⁹Parthians, Medes and Elamites; residents of Mesopotamia, Judea and Cappadocia, Pontus and Asia. ¹⁰Phrygia and Pamphylia, Egypt and the parts of Libya near Cyrene; visitors from Rome ¹¹(both Jews and converts to Judaism); Cretans and Arabs—we hear them declaring the wonders of God in our own tongues!" ¹²Amazed and perplexed, they asked one another, "What does this mean?"

¹³Some, however, made fun of them and said, "They have had too much wine."

Acts 2:1–13

LEADER

If you have more than seven in your group, divide into groups of four for the discussion time. Refer to the Summary and Study Notes at the end of this session as needed. If 30 minutes is not enough time to answer all of the questions in this section, conclude the Bible Study by answering question #7.

QUESTIONS FOR INTERACTION

1. Had you been present when the Holy Spirit came upon the disciples at Pentecost, who would you have been more like, those who were amazed by the wonders of God, or those who thought the disciples were drunk? Would you have always been in that group? How about when you were college age?

2. What two uncontrollable forces are used to represent the Holy Spirit in this passage (vv. 2–3)?

3. Why do you think God performed this miracle of having people speak in other tongues?
❐ To show his power.
❐ To break through cultural barriers.
❐ To show that he wanted an international church.
❐ Other_____.

Explain why you gave the answer you did.

4. How would you have answered if the "amazed and perplexed" people who were gathered for Pentecost had asked you, "What does this mean" (v. 12)?

5. If you were to share just one "wonder of God" (v. 11) that you have experienced, with a group like those gathered for Pentecost, what would it be?

6. What "barrier" do you most need to get past right now?
❐ The one between you and your children or grandchildren.
❐ The one between men and women.
❐ The one between nationalities.
❐ Other_____.

7. What message do you most urgently want to get across to someone in your life who "speaks another language"?

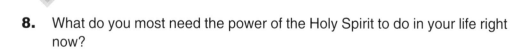 **GOING DEEPER:** *If your group has time and/or wants a challenge, go on to this question.*

8. What do you most need the power of the Holy Spirit to do in your life right now?

CARING TIME

15 Min.

APPLY THE LESSON AND PRAY FOR ONE ANOTHER

LEADER

Bring the group members back together and begin the Caring Time by sharing responses to all three questions. Be sure to take turns so everyone gets a chance to participate.

Take time now to share how God is working in your life and to pray for one another and support one another.

1. If you were to describe this past week of your life in terms of weather, what was it like: Sunny and warm? Cold? Scattered showers? Other? What is the forecast for the coming week?

2. What amazing thing has God done in your life that you would like to thank him for?

3. If you were to ask God for a miracle in your life today, what would it be?

P.S. *Add new group members to the Group Directory inside the front cover.*

NEXT WEEK

Today we saw the presence and power of the Holy Spirit transform the disciples from timid, unsure men in hiding into bold apostles, preaching the Gospel to anyone who would listen. Take a few moments each day in the coming week to seek the Holy Spirit's infilling power and see how God uses you to reach others for Christ. Next week we will study how the entire church was transformed into a caring, vibrant community for Christ. We will be reminded once again that this same Holy Spirit is available for each and every believer today, and the Holy Spirit who transforms us individually can also transform our groups into vibrant, caring Christian communities.

NOTES ON ACTS 2:1–13

Summary: The events of this chapter make up what is considered by most to be the birthday of the church. And a very important "guest" who showed up for the party was the Holy Spirit. From this moment forward the Holy Spirit was the driving force behind what became the church's phenomenal expansion throughout the Middle East and into Europe. When the Holy Spirit came into the room on this Pentecost, was this something entirely new? Not exactly. The Holy Spirit is part of God, and hence was not something invented or created at Pentecost. The Old Testament refers to the Holy Spirit, generally referring to "the Spirit" of God' or "the Spirit of the Lord" (see for instance Gen. 1:2; Ezek. 37:1). What was new at Pentecost was that this Spirit was made available to the church of Jesus Christ on a continuing basis.

In this story the disciples had come together for Pentecost. Christians sometimes get the mistaken impression that Pentecost has always been a day important only to Christians. However, it was originally an Old Testament feast holiday celebrated 50 days after the Passover. It was also called the "Feast of Weeks." It originally celebrated the end of the grain harvest, much like our Thanksgiving. But by New Testament times it also celebrated God's giving of the Law to Moses.

This story isn't just about the coming of the Holy Spirit on an Old Testament feast day. It was about a new kind of community. Previous to this time, faith communities had been almost exclusively made up of people of the same culture and national heritage. On this Pentecost was born a cross-cultural faith community. In a sense this story is a kind of "reverse tower of Babel" (Gen. 11:1–9). In that story people had tried to bring themselves together as one by building a tower under their own initiative and power. God responded by confusing their language, which drove them apart. Now, at Pentecost, God reversed the process. By miraculously helping everyone to understand one another's language, God brought people together in one Christian experience of faith and worship!

In this story then we see that right from the first, Christ's kingdom was multicultural. There were no "English only" equivalents here! God wanted everyone to understand what was happening in terms of the language with which they were familiar. The Gospel was too important a message to become garbled by a language barrier.

The end result of the events of Pentecost Sunday was that 3,000 people came to faith in Jesus Christ (2:41). The number of converts is not the only indicator of the presence of the Holy Spirit. There is also the number of people whose needs are cared for in the name of Jesus Christ, the number of ways the poor and oppressed are stood up for (Luke 4:16–21), and the number of ways the "seed" of the Gospel is spread (Matt. 13:1–23). But if acts of power are done, and if people's needs are addressed, and if the Gospel is preached, there will be converts. We won't be able to keep them away!

2:1 *the day of Pentecost.* This was the Feast of Harvest or Weeks (Ex. 23:16; Lev. 23:15–21; Deut. 16:9–12), held 50 days after Passover. Originally a kind of Thanksgiving Day for gathered crops, it came to be associated with the commemoration of the giving of the Law at Mount Sinai (Ex. 20:1–17). Jewish tradition held that when God gave the Law to Moses, a single voice spoke which was heard by all the nations of the world in their own language. Luke may be alluding to that in this story. Pentecost was a celebration to which thousands of Jews from all over the empire would attend.

2:2 *a violent wind.* In both Hebrew (the language in which the Old Testament was originally written) and Greek (the language in which the New Testament was originally written), the word translated as "Spirit" and "wind" and "breath" is all the same word. In Hebrew the word is *rhuah*. In Greek the word is *pneuma*. While one might think that this could lead to confusion, and it can, it also adds meaning. Is this "wind" from heaven truly a wind or is it the Spirit of God? Actually, it's both! Similarly, when God breathed into humankind the "breath" of life (Gen. 2:7), was it really the "breath" of life or the "Spirit" of life? Again, it was both! Note also that it was a violent wind that came at Pentecost. What does that say to us? It reminds us that while the Holy Spirit can bring peace to the soul, the Spirit is also a powerful force that we cannot expect to control or stifle. Even today violent winds like tornadoes and hurricanes frustrate human efforts at controlling them. Human power is humbled by such violent power. The Holy Spirit is also a power we cannot control.

2:3 *seemed to be tongues of fire.* Fire is often associated with divine appearances (Ex. 3:2; 19:18). John the Baptist said Jesus would baptize his followers with the Holy Spirit and fire (Luke 3:16), symbolizing the cleansing, purifying effect of the Spirit. What is important here is that tongues served as a sign to the crowds of a supernatural event, pointing to Jesus Christ as the way to salvation.

2:4 *filled with the Holy Spirit.* This phrase is found elsewhere (Acts 4:8,31; 13:52; Eph. 5:18) indicating a repeatable experience. Here, however, it is clearly associated with the baptism of the Spirit (Acts 1:5) which is an experience new converts enter into upon acceptance of Jesus as the Messiah (Acts 2:41).

2:5 *God-fearing Jews from every nation.* This was made possible because the Feast of Weeks (Pentecost) was one of the feasts where Jews would come from everywhere to celebrate. What a good time to initiate a church in which all peoples become one in Christ!

2:7 *Galileans.* Most of the church at this time consisted of people who had followed Jesus down from his home area of Galilee.

2:9–11 *Parthians, Medes, and Elamites ... Mesopotamia.* Present day Iran and Iraq, to the east of Jerusalem. These Jews traced their roots back to the Assyrian overthrow of Israel and the Babylonian overthrow of Judea seven and five centuries beforehand respectively. ***Judea.*** Either the immediate environs around Jerusalem are in view, or Luke is thinking of the days under David and Solomon when the land of Israel stretched from Egypt on the west to the Euphrates River on the east. ***Cappadocia, Pontus and Asia, Phrygia and Pamphylia.*** Present day Turkey to the north of Jerusalem. Much of Acts takes place in this region. ***Egypt ... Libya near Cyrene.*** To the west of Jerusalem on the northern coast of Africa. ***converts to Judaism.*** Judaism's high morality and developed spirituality attracted many Gentiles from other religions. ***Cretans.*** An island south of Greece in the Mediterranean Sea. ***Arabs.*** The Nabetean kingdom was south of Jerusalem with borders on Egypt and the Euphrates.

2:11 *the wonders of God.* The result of these "wonders" was that people were "amazed" (vv. 7,12), "perplexed" (v. 7) and "bewildered" (v. 6)—anything but bored! What happens when churches lose the Holy Spirit? Some imply that churches where the people show less emotion have lost the Spirit. But that is not necessarily the case. The best evidence of the Holy Spirit's presence is not emotional expression (although in some people the Spirit's presence does result in emotional expression), but the manifestation of acts of God's power. This means we need to be open to letting God do great things through us. And God can only do great things through us if we attempt great things for God.

THE COMMUNITY SHARES AND GROWS

SCRIPTURE ACTS 2:42–47

LAST WEEK

The coming of the Holy Spirit empowered the first believers to boldly proclaim the Gospel, as we studied in last week's session. Today we will consider how the Holy Spirit guided the early church and made it a place of learning, worshiping, praying, sharing and reaching out to others.

ICE-BREAKER   15 Min.
CONNECT WITH YOUR GROUP

LEADER

Choose one or two of the Ice-Breaker questions. If you have a new group member you may want to do all three. Remember to stick closely to the three-part agenda and the time allowed for each segment.

Sharing our time, feelings or possessions can be a joy and a struggle. Take some time now to share some of your own experiences with sharing.

1. When you were in junior high, which of your possessions were you most likely to share with friends?
   ❏ Clothes, like hats or sweatshirts.
   ❏ Records, tapes or CDs.
   ❏ Other _____.

2. If you were asked to share what you have with a group right now, what possession would you be most hesitant to share?

3. What are you most likely to eat when you have a meal with friends?

BIBLE STUDY

READ SCRIPTURE AND DISCUSS

30 Min.

LEADER

Have a member of the group, selected ahead of time, read aloud the passage. Then discuss the questions that follow, breaking up into smaller subgroups as necessary.

After the coming of the Holy Spirit at Pentecost the church grew and thrived. Many were drawn to the new Christians because of their love and generosity. Read Acts 2:42–47 and imagine yourself in this beautiful fellowship.

The Fellowship of the Jerusalem Church

⁴²They devoted themselves to the apostles' teaching and to the fellowship, to the breaking of bread and to prayer. ⁴³Everyone was filled with awe, and many wonders and miraculous signs were done by the apostles. ⁴⁴All the believers were together and had everything in common. ⁴⁵Selling their possessions and goods, they gave to anyone as he had need. ⁴⁶Every day they continued to meet together in the temple courts. They broke bread in their homes and ate together with glad and sincere hearts, ⁴⁷praising God and enjoying the favor of all the people. And the Lord added to their number daily those who were being saved.

Acts 2:42–47

LEADER

Refer to the Summary and Study Notes at the conclusion of this session as needed. If 30 minutes is not enough time to answer all of the questions in this section, conclude the Bible Study by answering question #7.

QUESTIONS FOR INTERACTION

1. What is the closest you have come to experiencing a fellowship like these believers had together?

2. If you had to pinpoint the most important key to what made this Christian fellowship "work," what would it be?

3. How do you relate to the early church's practice of having "everything in common"? How do you think you would get along in a community that practiced this early form of socialism?

4. Which of the factors referred to in this passage is the greatest strength of the body of believers with whom you now worship?
❏ Joint study.
❏ Sharing food and fellowship.
❏ Praying together.
❏ Caring for each other's needs.
❏ Joyful celebration.
❏ Other _____.

5. Which of the factors in question #4 is missing most in your present relationship with other believers?

6. If your church began a ministry to meet the greatest need of the people in your community, what need would that be and what would your church need to "sell" or sacrifice to minister to that need?

7. How does the "harvest" of the church in Acts, where the Lord "added to their number daily those who were being saved," compare to that of your own church? What do you see in this passage that might account for any disparity?

GOING DEEPER: *If your group has time and/or wants a challenge, go on to this question.*

8. Should the church today be doing "miraculous signs"? What constitutes a "miraculous sign"?

CARING TIME   15 Min.
APPLY THE LESSON AND PRAY FOR ONE ANOTHER

. . . .

LEADER

Begin the Caring Time by having group members take turns sharing responses to all three questions. Be sure to save at least the last five minutes for a time of group prayer. Remember to include a prayer for the empty chair when concluding the prayer time.

Following the example of the early church in Acts 2, devote this time now to praying for one another and for your own special concerns.

1. How could you reach out and meet the need of a neighbor, coworker, family member, friend or stranger this week? How could your church help?

2. How comfortable do you feel sharing your needs and struggles with this group? What would make it easier for you?

3. Finish this sentence: "The area of need where this group could minister to me this week is ..." Then pray for these areas.

NEXT WEEK

Today we were given a glimpse into the life of the early church and how the Holy Spirit inspired the first believers to reach out and meet the needs of others. We were reminded what an incredible witness this kind of sharing can be and how the church can grow through generosity and love. In the coming week, take some time to write a note of appreciation to someone who has met a need in your life. Next week we will see how Peter continued this spirit of generosity by healing a crippled beggar, and using this miracle to spread the Good News of Jesus.

NOTES ON ACTS 2:42–47

Summary: When a company first builds something, like a new model of car, they first build a prototype. This demonstrates how the new model can perform and what it needs to look like. It also serves as a model from which to build the cars to follow. For instance, engineers have been working for decades on the hybrid electric-gasoline powered cars that have come out just recently for the general market. Similarly, the church that was built through the Holy Spirit in Jerusalem during the infancy of the Christian faith can be seen as a prototype for churches down through the ages. That doesn't mean that every church needs to function exactly like the church described in Acts. (For instance, most churches will not "have all things in common.") However, we can still learn some important elements that ought to be present in every church and its ministry. There is no better passage for studying these elements than this passage from the second chapter of Acts (along with its parallel passage in 4:32–37). It is a summary statement for what the common life of the church was like at this time.

This passage basically underlines both the "deeds of power" and the kind of community that was created by the amazing events that happened because of the coming of the Holy Spirit at Pentecost. The church of this time grew because the Holy Spirit empowered the believers to become a deeply caring community, where God was able to do great deeds. These great deeds were done through a church that cared about human needs of every kind, from physical to relational to spiritual.

The first believers were not just a caring community, however. They were also a studying and a worshiping community. In order for us to act with the caring of Jesus Christ, we must first study to learn of Christ's life and how he showed caring. In order to do deeds of power, we must turn to God in worship, receiving the power of God, and giving God the glory for our victories. Worship was not something the early Christians did just once a week, either. Worship was their way of life ("Everyone was filled with awe", v. 43). They met every day in the temple courts (v. 46), but not as a refuge from the world. They met to find renewal so they could go into the world with their deeds of love and message of Good News in Jesus Christ. Such a way of life is what made this church exemplary.

2:42 The four components of the church's life here may represent what occurred at their gatherings. ***teaching.*** The foundation for the church's life was the instruction given by the apostles as the representatives of Jesus. A true Christian fellowship cannot exist without focusing on a common faith in Jesus Christ. When we have a common understanding of God's love and a passion for Christ, the bonds between us are set even stronger. ***fellowship.*** Literally, "sharing." While this may include the aspect of sharing to meet material needs (v. 45), it most likely means their common participation in the Spirit as they worshiped together (1 Cor. 12). ***the breaking of bread.*** This refers to the Lord's Supper in which they remembered his death (Luke 22:19–20), and recognized his presence among them (Luke 24:30–31). ***to prayer.*** Literally, "the prayers." This may refer to set times and forms of prayer, as was the practice of the Jews.

2:43–47 The picture of the church is one of continual growth (vv. 43,47), marked by generous sharing (vv. 44–45) and joyful worship and fellowship (vv. 46–47). The worship at the temple continued as before, since the line dividing Christianity from Judaism had not yet been drawn. Christians simply saw their faith as the natural end of what the Jewish faith had always declared.

2:44–45 *everything in common.* While this was a primitive form of socialism, it certainly did not include the oppressive totalitarianism or denial of God found in many modern forms. It was simply an outgrowth of the intense love people had for each other through Jesus Christ. They believed that in Christ each person's need should in some sense become everyone's need. While one might question the political practicality of sharing property, the attitude behind it was exemplary. The people decided to take the attitude, "Your need is my need." Then they gave caring to each other that went beyond smiles and well-wishing. It should be noted, however, that while sometimes this practice of sharing posses-

sions worked quite well (4:36–37), at other times people were victimized by greed and deception (5:1–11).

2:46 *They broke bread in their homes and ate together.* These early Christians gave each other the precious gift of their time. In contrast, our society is becoming more and more isolated. People today refer to "cocooning"—staying in the isolated "cocoon" of one's home and not coming out unless absolutely necessary (which isn't often, given all that can be done on the Internet)! People today are hungry, however, for intimacy and friendship, and that takes time. We need to understand that to get the kind of community they had in the early church, we must invest our time in each other.

2:47 *And the Lord added.* Growth in the church was a natural result of the believers' love, fellowship and commitment to the apostles' teaching. Since most churches today, at least those in the most economically privileged sections of western civilization, don't come close to achieving this kind of success in evangelism, we need to consider what caused this growth. In verse 43 we read that "many signs and wonders were being done." This was another way of saying "miracles." In other words, people's needs were being fulfilled. Just like Jesus' healing ministry created a buzz among the populace (Mark 1:40–45; John 6:1–2), so also did the healing ministry of the early church. We debate back and forth between various denominations and Christian perspectives whether this kind of miraculous healing ministry can be done in the church of today, with our understanding of modern medicine. Rather than debating, we should be focusing on need fulfillment. In the church of this time, medicine was not nearly as advanced as it is today, and so this healing ministry was filling a desperate need that the people had. What similar needs do people have today that the church can address? A church that wants to follow the example of the church in Acts needs to ask that question and seek God's guidance on ways to respond to those needs.

SESSION 4
PETER HEALS A MAN

SCRIPTURE ACTS 3:1–16

LAST WEEK

Last week we looked at the beautiful fellowship and ministry of the early church. We were reminded of the importance of reaching out and meeting the needs of others as a powerful way to share the love of Jesus. Today we will see Peter reach out and meet the physical and spiritual needs of a beggar.

ICE-BREAKER   15 Min.
CONNECT WITH YOUR GROUP

LEADER

Choose one, two or all three of the Ice-Breaker questions. Welcome and introduce new group members.

Help can come in many ways, and sometimes when we least expect it. Takes turns sharing how you found or needed help when you were in those difficult preteen or teen years.

1. What did you spend your money on when you were in the seventh grade? How did you get your spending money?
   ❒ Asked your parents.
   ❒ Got an allowance.
   ❒ Had a job.

2. What was the most "crippling" problem you had as an adolescent?
   ❒ Shyness.
   ❒ Learning disabilities.
   ❒ Stubbornness.
   ❒ Rebelliousness.
   ❒ Other _____.

3. Where did you used to "hang out" in the seventh grade? Where were your friends most likely to find you?

BIBLE STUDY — 30 Min.
READ SCRIPTURE AND DISCUSS

LEADER

Select two members of the group ahead of time to read the Scripture passage. Have one read the part of Luke, the narrator, and the other read the part of Peter. Then divide into subgroups as needed for discussion of the Questions for Interaction.

In today's Scripture passage we see an ordinary day turn into the extraordinary for a man crippled from birth. Peter's faith and willingness to act becomes a living testimony to the power of God and the truth of salvation through believing in Jesus. Read Acts 3:1–16 and recall this wonderful miracle of healing.

Peter Heals a Man with a Disability

Luke: **3** *One day Peter and John were going up to the temple at the time of prayer—at three in the afternoon. [2]Now a man crippled from birth was being carried to the temple gate called Beautiful, where he was put every day to beg from those going into the temple courts. [3]When he saw Peter and John about to enter, he asked them for money. [4]Peter looked straight at him, as did John.*

Peter: *Then Peter said, "Look at us!"*

Luke: *[5]So the man gave them his attention, expecting to get something from them.*

Peter: *[6]Then Peter said, "Silver or gold I do not have, but what I have I give you. In the name of Jesus Christ of Nazareth, walk."*

Luke: *[7]Taking him by the right hand, he helped him up, and instantly the man's feet and ankles became strong. [8]He jumped to his feet and began to walk. Then he went with them into the temple courts, walking and jumping, and praising God. [9]When all the people saw him walking and praising God, [10]they recognized him as the same man who used to sit begging at the temple gate called Beautiful, and they were filled with wonder and amazement at what had happened to him.*
[11]While the beggar held on to Peter and John, all the people were astonished and came running to them in the place called Solomon's Colonnade.

Peter: *[12]When Peter saw this, he said to them: "Men of Israel, why does this surprise you? Why do you stare at us as if by our own power or godliness we had made this man walk? [13]The God of Abraham, Isaac and Jacob, the God of our fathers, has glorified his servant Jesus. You handed him over to be killed, and you disowned him before Pilate, though he had decided to let him go. [14]You disowned the Holy and Righteous One and asked that a murderer be released to you. [15]You killed the author of life, but God raised him from the dead. We are witnesses of this. [16]By faith in the name of Jesus, this man whom you see and know was made strong. It is Jesus' name and the faith that comes through him that has given this complete healing to him, as you can all see."*
Acts 3:1–16

QUESTIONS FOR INTERACTION

1. In the midst of the struggles you sometimes face in life, what kind of help do you normally expect from others?
❏ None at all.
❏ Minimal.
❏ A lot.
❏ Whatever it takes.

2. What do you normally do when a beggar asks you for money?

3. Why was this man specifically put near the gate of the temple in order to beg?

4. How did this beggar react to his healing? Who does he thank?

5. Why does Peter take special care to let people know who deserved credit for the healing?

6. What has God done for you that has caused you to jump and praise God?

7. What "disability" (physical, relational or spiritual) do you have right now that you need to entrust to God for healing?

GOING DEEPER: *If your group has time and/or wants a challenge, go on to this question.*

8. Peter spoke of how the people of the time rejected Jesus, who was sent from God. How can we avoid making the same mistake of rejecting those whom God is speaking through today?

CARING TIME   15 Min.

APPLY THE LESSON AND PRAY FOR ONE ANOTHER

LEADER

Be sure to save at least 15 minutes for this important time. After sharing responses to all three questions and asking for prayer requests, close in a time of group prayer.

Take some time now to bring each other healing and hope by sharing prayer requests and special concerns. Before closing in prayer, take turns sharing your answers to the following questions.

1. How could you bring God's healing touch to someone in the coming week?

2. How are you doing at inviting others to this group?

3. The man in this story expected to get something from the disciples. What do you expect to get from this group? Are you getting it?

NEXT WEEK

In today's lesson we were reminded of the healing power of God and how we, as Christians, can pass that healing along to others. Peter and John had been made whole again through the sacrifice and blood of Jesus and they wanted that more than anything for others. In the coming week, pray daily for a person you know who needs spiritual healing, and show your concern for that person in some way. Next week we will again learn from Peter and John as they stand up for their faith before the Sanhedrin and boldly proclaim what God has done for them.

NOTES ON ACTS 3:1–16

Summary: Acts 2:43 refers to many "signs and wonders" that were being done by the apostles, and here we have the first specific example. Even as Jesus healed the sick and the lame, now Peter and the apostles show evidence of the same gift. But they make it clear that this gift is not due to a natural ability, or to their own righteousness (v. 12). It is a special gift given by God and used to point to God's glory (vv. 13–17).

This story speaks to how we can really help others. Our first inclination is to give money to help "people in need." That certainly can be an important way of helping. People who have gone through a run of hard luck often need just a little financial boost to pull out of a tough spot. But there is also a kind of financial giving that just encourages dependence. It is possible that this beggar was in that kind of situation. He thought that he would never be anything other than a beggar who couldn't walk and do things for himself. After all, he had been that way since his birth. However, Peter perceived that there was potential here for a more complete kind of helping. He didn't have money to give, but he perceived that money was not what the man really needed at this point. He needed to get away from a dependent lifestyle, and the gift he needed to help him do that was the gift of faith in Jesus Christ. Peter helped him in two ways: (1) He pointed the man to the source of healing—"In the name of Jesus Christ of Nazareth, walk" (v. 6); and (2) He gave him the physical assistance that he needed to get started—"Taking him by the right hand, he helped him up ..." (v. 7). In other words, he didn't just give him sage advice, tell him about Jesus and figure that was all he needed. Peter pointed to Jesus as the source of healing and he did all he could to help the man onto his own two feet.

The apostles believed that healing was part of their ministry, and that healings should be expected when you rely upon the power of God. People who see such healings occur should not ever be surprised (v. 12). That is the kind of faith that built the early church.

3:1 *the time of prayer.* The two daily times of sacrifice and prayer at the temple were in the early morning and around 3 P.M.

3:2 *the temple gate called Beautiful.* It is uncertain which of the temple's many gates had this name, but it was apparently near Solomon's Colonnade (v. 11) on the eastern side of the temple. Beggars would gather about the temple in hopes of receiving alms since charity was a major part of Jewish piety.

3:3–5 Almsgiving was an impersonal act as the giver simply dropped a coin into the hands of a person who was already looking for the next person to ask for help. The man probably simply called out for alms without paying attention to whom he was talking. In contrast, Peter and John break through his routine by insisting that he pay attention to them. In Christ, caring for those in need is relational. The homeless and poor can hunger as much for someone to look them in the eye and relate to them as persons, as they do for food. When Peter did this, the man's expectations for a generous gift must have been raised. It may be that at this point he recognized Peter and John as among the leaders of the band of people who had recently pledged their loyalty to Jesus.

3:6 *Silver or gold I do not have.* This statement implies that money is not what is truly valuable anyway. To experience life fully is surely more valuable than money, and the healing that Peter was about to do would help this man live more fully. This is but one example of the fact that what Christ gives is far more valuable than what the world gives. *In the name of Jesus Christ* By the authority and presence of Jesus, who so often healed the sick, this man is healed. In the name was the power of the person. This was so much so that even those who were not Jesus' followers sought to heal using his name.

3:8 *jumped to his feet ... praising God.* The beggar makes no attempt to hide his excitement. The fact that he *jumps* to his feet is both a sign of excitement and a sign of how complete the healing was, given that jumping takes far more leg strength than simply rising to one's feet (Isa. 35:6).

3:9–10 The celebration of the man draws a crowd that wonders how it could be that he is suddenly healed. *they recognized him as the same man.* This was not some hoax where the disciples brought in a stranger who claimed to be disabled, and then rose on cue. The people knew this man and knew that he had been unable to walk since birth. From this day forward this man's ability to walk would be a testimony to all who had seen him begging for so long.

3:11 *Solomon's Colonnade.* This was a long porch extending along the eastern wall of the outer court of the temple. It was the typical gathering place for the early Jewish Christians (5:12).

3:12 *Why do you stare at us?* As at Pentecost (2:15), Peter is eager to direct attention away from the immediate phenomenon to the significance behind what has happened.

3:13 *The God of Abraham, Isaac and Jacob.* This was a common way of referring to God as the one who had entered into covenant faithfulness with Israel. *his servant Jesus.* The "Servant Songs" of Isaiah (Isa. 42:1ff; 49:1–3, 5, 8; 50:4–9 and especially Isa. 52:13–53:12) describe the mission of the Messiah most fully, as well as teach his suffering, death and exaltation.

3:14 *the Holy and Righteous One.* The Holy One of God was a designation of the Messiah (Mark 1:24; John 6:69; Rev. 3:7). It was used in Luke 1:35 as a description of how the child of Mary would belong in a special way to God, just like the Servant of Isaiah (Isa. 52:13–53:12). The Righteous One also is rooted in the same song (Isa. 53:11). Together these terms accent the uniqueness and uprightness of Jesus.

3:15 *the author of life.* The word for "author" is translated in Acts 5:31 as "Prince." It has the idea of a leader, a founder and ruler (Heb. 2:10; 12:2). In Aramaic, the word for "life" and "salvation" is the same.

3:16 In the Greek, this is a difficult sentence, but its point is clear—it is because of faith (whether the man's or Peter's is unclear) in the presence, power and character of Jesus that this man has been healed.

Session 5
Facing the Sanhedrin

Scripture Acts 4:1–22

LAST WEEK

In last week's session, we were reminded of the power of God to heal us and meet our needs. When Peter healed the crippled beggar he wanted everyone to understand that God was working through him. As he said in Acts 3:16, "By faith in the name of Jesus, this man whom you see and know was made strong." This week we will see Peter once again draw upon his faith in Jesus as he and John are brought before the Jewish rulers and elders to defend this act of healing.

ICE-BREAKER   15 Min.
Connect with your Group

LEADER

To help new group members get acquainted, remember to do all three Ice-Breaker questions.

Is it right to obey or not to obey? That is the question! Adolescence is often a time of struggle against authority. Take turns sharing some experiences you had with authority in high school.

1. When you were in high school, what were you most likely to get "called on the carpet" for?
    ❏ Skipping school.
    ❏ Lying to your parents.
    ❏ Not practicing your musical instrument.
    ❏ Not telling people where you were going.
    ❏ Other _____.

2. Who was your foremost authority when you were in high school—the one you followed whenever there was any conflict concerning the direction you would go?

❐ Your parent(s).

❐ A teacher or counselor.

❐ Your peers.

❐ Yourself.

❐ God.

❐ Your horoscope.

3. What could you "not stop talking about" when you were in high school?

❐ Who was going with whom.

❐ Sex.

❐ Sports.

❐ Your favorite music group.

❐ Other _____.

BIBLE STUDY   30 Min.
READ SCRIPTURE AND DISCUSS

LEADER

Have a member of the group, selected ahead of time, read aloud the Scripture passage. Then discuss the Questions for Interaction, dividing into smaller subgroups of four.

Today we find Peter and John being questioned and threatened by the Jewish rulers and elders. They are called upon to explain their actions and words, and to stop speaking out for Jesus. Read Acts 4:1–22 and observe how Peter, inspired by the Holy Spirit, eloquently responds to the Sanhedrin's demands.

Peter and John Before the Sanhedrin

4 The priests and the captain of the temple guard and the Sadducees came up to Peter and John while they were speaking to the people. ²They were greatly disturbed because the apostles were teaching the people and proclaiming in Jesus the resurrection of the dead. ³They seized Peter and John, and because it was evening, they put them in jail until the next day. ⁴But many who heard the message believed, and the number of men grew to about five thousand.

⁵The next day the rulers, elders and teachers of the law met in Jerusalem. ⁶Annas the high priest was there, and so were Caiaphas, John, Alexander and the other men of the high priest's family. ⁷They had Peter and John brought before them and began to question them: "By what power or what name did you do this?"

⁸Then Peter, filled with the Holy Spirit, said to them: "Rulers and elders of the people! [9]If we are being called to account today for an act of kindness shown to a cripple and are asked how he was healed, [10]then know this, you and all the people of Israel: It is by the name of Jesus Christ of Nazareth, whom you crucified but whom God raised from the dead, that this man stands before you healed. [11]He is

" 'the stone you builders rejected,
which has become the capstone.'

[12]Salvation is found in no one else, for there is no other name under heaven given to men by which we must be saved."

[13]When they saw the courage of Peter and John and realized that they were unschooled, ordinary men, they were astonished and they took note that these men had been with Jesus. [14]But since they could see the man who had been healed standing there with them, there was nothing they could say. [15]So they ordered them to withdraw from the Sanhedrin and then conferred together. [16]"What are we going to do with these men?" they asked. "Everybody living in Jerusalem knows they have done an outstanding miracle, and we cannot deny it. [17]But to stop this thing from spreading any further among the people, we must warn these men to speak no longer to anyone in this name."

[18]Then they called them in again and commanded them not to speak or teach at all in the name of Jesus. [19]But Peter and John replied, "Judge for yourselves whether it is right in God's sight to obey you rather than God. [20]For we cannot help speaking about what we have seen and heard."

[21]After further threats they let them go. They could not decide how to punish them, because all the people were praising God for what had happened. [22]For the man who was miraculously healed was over forty years old.

Acts 4:1–22

QUESTIONS FOR INTERACTION

LEADER

Refer to the Summary and Study Notes at the end of the session as needed. If 30 minutes is not enough time to answer all of the questions in this section, conclude the Bible Study by answering question #8.

1. Faced with this directive from authorities, if you were Peter or John, how likely would you have been to "do what you were told"?

2. What do you think upset the Sanhedrin the most?
   ❒ That the disciples were teaching the resurrection (see Notes on v. 2).
   ❒ That the disciples were proclaiming Jesus, one whom they had condemned, as the Messiah.
   ❒ That the disciples were getting more attention from the people than they were.
   ❒ Other _____.

3. What was the significance of the fact that Peter and John were unschooled, ordinary men (see Note on v. 13)?

4. What was the hardest fact for the Sanhedrin to argue against?

5. Why did the Sanhedrin have a difficult time following through with their threats and punishing Peter and John?

6. When do you have the most difficult time obeying God over the other voices around you?
❐ When the voices are those of your friends and/or family members.
❐ When the voices are those of your bosses at work.
❐ When the voices are those of the government.
❐ Other _____.

7. When has something happened to you recently that you couldn't help speaking about to others? Why was this event so compelling?

8. When has God done something for you that was so wonderful you had the same compulsion to speak about it as you did during the event you mentioned in question #7? If you have never had such an experience, what would God need to do for you to have this sense of compulsion?

GOING DEEPER: *If your group has time and/or wants a challenge, go on to this question.*

9. When, if ever, is a Christian justified in defying a governing authority (see vv. 19–20; see also Rom. 13:1–7)?

CARING TIME   15 Min.

APPLY THE LESSON AND PRAY FOR ONE ANOTHER

· ·

LEADER

Encourage everyone to participate in this important time and be sure that each group member is receiving prayer support. Continue to pray for the empty chair in the closing group prayer.

Remember that this time is for developing and expressing your caring for each other as group members. Take turns sharing your responses to the questions below. Conclude by sharing prayer requests and praying for each other's needs.

1. What problem or difficulty in your life do you need to submit to God's authority?

2. Share with the group a challenge that you are facing this week.

3. Peter and John had a great victory over the Sanhedrin. Is there a spiritual victory from this last week you would like to share?

NEXT WEEK

In today's Scripture, Peter and John demonstrated what to do when we are faced with the question of obeying God or obeying man. In the coming week, pray for the boldness to stand up for your faith in all situations. As we continue our study of Acts next week, we will consider how the early church handles a conflict and is an example to us of Christian service and love.

NOTES ON ACTS 4:1–22

Summary: If God is your highest authority, how do you relate to the authority of your own government? That question arises in this story, and has been an important question many times throughout history. There have been several approaches Christians have taken to answering this question. One is to fully equate what the governing authorities do with God's will. These authorities speak for God. Period. End of discussion. This was the approach in medieval Europe under the doctrine of the divine right of kings, and it also exemplifies the attitude many Americans have taken. "God is not only on our side, but he speaks through our leaders." If such is true, then any conflict between what God wants and what our political leaders say is inconceivable. Most Christians today, however, have seen enough conflicts between what the Bible says God wants, and what our political leaders do and ask for, to at least seriously doubt this perspective.

Another approach some people take is to defer to the government in most, if not all cases. "After all," the argument might go, "can we really be sure enough of what God wants to defy our own government?" But as we look at this story from Acts and see the behavior of Peter and John, we would have to say that they thought they could be sure of what God wanted. "Judge for yourselves whether it is right in God's sight to obey you rather than God. For we cannot help speaking about what we have seen and heard" (vv. 19–20). They knew that God had called them to witness to the Gospel and when their authorities told them not to, the disciples knew whom to obey. They are even more direct in Acts 5:29, where they say, "We must obey God rather than men!" They had the confidence and the courage to say that when the government goes against what God has specifically called us to do, we must obey God.

The disciples did, however, avoid another option that Christians sometimes have taken—complete defiance of and non-cooperation with the government. They didn't lead any tax rebellions. They sought to be obedient on matters not related to the faith. The writings of Paul in Romans 13 particularly urge good citizenship. But what Peter and John and the others knew first and foremost was that they were part of a greater kingdom—the kingdom of God, and that kingdom demanded primary allegiance.

4:1 *the captain of the temple guard.* A high-ranking official who had the responsibility of maintaining order in the temple. *the Sadducees.* The Sadducees were a wealthy group who believed only in the first five books of the Old Testament and denied the resurrection of the dead. The Sadducees play a leading role in the opposition to the church in Acts (see 23:6–8).

4:2 The Sadducees considered teaching to be a priestly right alone. To further upset things, the disciples were preaching the resurrection, a doctrine which the Sadducees did not believe.

4:6 *Annas the high priest.* Caiaphas, Annas' son-in-law, was the official high priest since Annas had been removed from office in A.D. 14 by the Roman procurator. However, within Jewish circles Annas retained both the title and much of the real power.

4:9 There may be more than a touch of irony in Peter's reference to the "crime" for which they were detained!

4:10 Although the Sanhedrin represented the highest level of authority and power in the Jewish social and political structure, they do not intimidate Peter. He confronts them with the fact that the miracle was not a product of sorcery but of faith in the power of Jesus, the Messiah, whom they had officially condemned to death a few weeks before. Again, the apostolic message stresses three central facts about Jesus: (1) although he was crucified, God raised him from death and exalted him as the Messiah (2:32–36; 3:13–15); (2) he continues to be present and active among those who trust in him (2:33; 3:16); and (3) the promise of salvation from sin is for those who will respond in faith to him (2:38–39; 3:19–20; 4:12).

4:11 While Psalm 118:22 originally referred to the exaltation of Israel among the nations that despised her, Peter interprets it in reference to the rejection of Jesus the Messiah by the Jewish leaders. The "stone" they despised would turn out to occupy the crowning point of God's building! This passage is quoted as well in 1 Peter 2:7 and alluded to in Ephesians 2:20.

4:12 Peter applies verse 11 by insisting that Jesus, whom they have rejected, is indeed the keystone in God's whole plan of salvation. *Salvation.* The Greek word for healing and salvation is the same, which allows Peter to make an easy transition from discussing the condition of the formerly crippled man to the spiritual state of the members of the Sanhedrin. The point is clear: either they repent and believe so that they may experience God's salvation, or they can persist in their rejection of Jesus and forfeit the very hope for which Israel had so long awaited.

4:13 The Sanhedrin not only realizes that Peter and John are disciples of Jesus, but also the boldness with which Peter speaks is all too reminiscent of the way Jesus spoke with arguments and objections that left his opponents' arguments in shambles (Luke 20:19,26,40). Luke probably intends this as another example of Jesus at work through his Spirit in the apostles (compare v. 14 with Luke 21:15). *unschooled, ordinary men.* These two Greek words refer to people ignorant of the Torah or Jewish Law. As fishermen by trade, Peter and John certainly never had the formal rabbinical training that many members of the Sanhedrin would have had.

4:15 How Luke got this inside information is uncertain, although at least one member of the council was a believer in Jesus and may have been Luke's source of information (Luke 23:50ff). *then conferred together.* It is interesting to contrast the response of the Sanhedrin under pressure to that of the disciples (Acts 4:24ff): the Sanhedrin "confer together" whereas the disciples pray.

4:16–17 Recognizing the irrefutable fact that the man was healed and the widespread popular support for the disciples (v. 21), the Sanhedrin realized there was little they could do at this point except try to use their power and status to intimidate the disciples into silence. They may still have feared a popular uprising that would bring down the harsh military might of the Romans (John 11:48), or they may more personally have feared the reaction of the people against them if this belief about Jesus as the Messiah got too widespread.

4:18 One can imagine the somber, threatening tones as the command of the Sanhedrin was given to Peter and John.

4:19–20 Peter and John, whether they are facing the council alone or together, both assert that the council has overstepped its bounds. Since the Sanhedrin set itself against God and his Messiah, the disciples have no choice but to ignore their commands and remain faithful to the Messiah. This response serves as a check on Paul's general principle about submission to government in Romans 13:1–7. Paul's point there is to correct notions that "freedom in Christ" means Christians have the right to ignore civil laws and authority: instead he asserts that since government is ordained of God to keep order and peace, normally the Christian ought to be the most responsible of citizens. But when government stubbornly defies God and his ways (as the Sanhedrin did here), then responsible resistance is demanded as a part of faithfulness to the authority of God. When such resistance is necessary is a difficult decision sometimes, and one considering it must consult the Spirit's guidance.

SESSION 6
SEVEN CHOSEN TO SERVE

SCRIPTURE   ACTS 6:1–7

LAST WEEK

Obeying God above all else and boldly speaking out for him is something we considered in last week's session as we studied the example of Peter and John defending their faith before the Sanhedrin. Today we will consider how the early church handles a conflict and begins a ministry of service to those in need.

ICE-BREAKER   15 Min.
CONNECT WITH YOUR GROUP

LEADER

Choose one or two of the Ice-Breaker questions. If you have a new group member you may want to do all three. Remember to stick closely to the three-part agenda and the time allowed for each segment.

Complaining is a pastime that many people have down to an art! Sometimes these complaints can result in positive changes, while at other times they can be divisive and hurtful. Take turns sharing how you have resolved complaints in the past.

1. When you were in high school, what group were you most likely to have a complaint about?
    ❏ The jocks.
    ❏ The popular kids.
    ❏ The teachers.
    ❏ The druggies.

How did you resolve your differences, if at all?

2. What are people in the household where you live today most likely to complain about?

❑ Food choices.

❑ Persons monopolizing the phone or computer.

❑ Other people's clutter.

How do you resolve those complaints?

3. When have you felt like you were "getting the short end of the stick" in a church situation? What did you do about it?

BIBLE STUDY   30 Min.
READ SCRIPTURE AND DISCUSS

LEADER

Select a member of the group ahead of time to read aloud the passage. Then discuss the Questions for Interaction, dividing into subgroups of four or five.

Yes, even the early church had conflicts to resolve! Today we will see how the disciples handled a problem between the Grecian Jews and the Hebraic Jews. Read Acts 6:1–7 and note the results of the solution to this problem.

Seven Chosen to Serve

6 In those days when the number of disciples was increasing, the Grecian Jews among them complained against the Hebraic Jews because their widows were being overlooked in the daily distribution of food. ²So the Twelve gathered all the disciples together and said, "It would not be right for us to neglect the ministry of the word of God in order to wait on tables. ³Brothers, choose seven men from among you who are known to be full of the Spirit and wisdom. We will turn this responsibility over to them ⁴and will give our attention to prayer and the ministry of the word."

⁵This proposal pleased the whole group. They chose Stephen, a man full of faith and of the Holy Spirit; also Philip, Procorus, Nicanor, Timon, Parmenas, and Nicolas from Antioch, a convert to Judaism. ⁶They presented these men to the apostles, who prayed and laid their hands on them.

⁷So the word of God spread. The number of disciples in Jerusalem increased rapidly, and a large number of priests became obedient to the faith.

Acts 6:1–7

QUESTIONS FOR INTERACTION

LEADER

Refer to the Summary and Study Notes at the conclusion of this session as needed. If 30 minutes is not enough time to answer all of the questions in this section, conclude the Bible Study by answering question #7.

1. Had you been one of the Twelve, how would you have most likely handled this conflict?
    ❐ Said, "Just deal with it!".
    ❐ Set up an investigative committee.
    ❐ Taken one side or the other.
    ❐ Done what the apostles did.
    ❐ Other _____.

2. Why is it significant that those selected to these positions all had Greek names (see note on verse 5)?

3. What special gifts were these men to have in order to do the ministry to which they would be assigned (see v. 3)?

4. Why did the twelve "lay their hands on" these new church leaders (see note on verse 6)?

5. Where do you see "cultural clashes" like this one in the church today? What needs to be done to get past cultural differences and be part of one fellowship that cares for one another?

6. Who is being neglected in your church today? What can you do to correct that situation?

7. What special ministry might God be calling you to at this time, as he called the seven men in this story?

GOING DEEPER: *If your group has time and/or wants a challenge, go on to this question.*

8. What is the best way to determine whom God has gifted to do certain tasks? How can the church do better than just grabbing whatever warm body that is available?

CARING TIME 15 Min.

APPLY THE LESSON AND PRAY FOR ONE ANOTHER

LEADER

Be sure to save at least 15 minutes for this time of prayer and encouragement. Continue to encourage group members to invite new people to the group.

After sharing your responses to the questions below, close by praying for one another and the concerns that have been shared.

1. What "complaint" or concern do you have that you would like the Holy Spirit's guidance and wisdom in resolving?

2. What need do you have that has been neglected of late?

3. Pray for the challenges and the possible ministries (question #7, above) that group members shared about.

NEXT WEEK

Today we were encouraged by the example of the early believers and how they handled a potentially divisive situation. In the coming week, write down any complaints or criticisms you have and pray for a wise solution to each problem. Next week we will also be encouraged by the example of Stephen, "a man full of God's grace and power" (6:8). Stephen paid the ultimate penalty for defending his faith, but through his final speech and martyrdom he has inspired people throughout the ages to look to Jesus for salvation.

NOTES ON ACTS 6:1–7

Summary: Sometimes we are tempted to over idealize the early church, as if it were the perfect Christian fellowship. Certainly, when we look at passages like the one we have already studied in Acts 2:42–47, and its "echo" in Acts 4:32–37, we realize that the fellowship of the early church had a lot going for them. On the other hand, they also had problems to deal with, and one of these is described in Acts 6:1–7.

This passage tells us that these events happened "when the number of disciples was increasing" (v. 1). This reminds us again that the early church was a fast-growing body. But there is a misunderstanding that church growth only brings conditions that Christians like and welcome. It can also bring some conditions that people often don't like, namely (1) change and (2) new cultures with the possibility of conflict. In this passage, the conflict that erupts is between the Grecian Jews and the Hebraic Jews. The Grecian Jews were followers of Christ, but they were Jews that had lived in and adapted to Greek culture. The Hebraic Jews were Jews who had not made such a cultural adaptation. We can see such a conflict today in places like the Arab or Asian countries where some people follow the traditional culture and some are "westernized." What were some of the areas where these cultures clashed? The more traditional Hebrews would have looked down on every aspect of Greek culture, and hence probably also on the Jews who were influenced by Greek culture. The Hellenists would revere Scripture, but also would have some knowledge of and respect for Greek philosophy. As there are clashes today between traditionalists and westernized people in Arab countries and Israel, so these groups would have clashed then. However, what brought them together at all was Jesus Christ. In no other group of the time were people brought together with the kind of differences that were in the church.

The cultural clash resulted in the Grecian Jews feeling that their widows were being neglected. In order to address this problem the twelve disciples got together and decided to delegate taking care of the problem to a new classification of church leader. The Twelve said, "It would not be right for us to neglect the ministry of the word of God in order to wait on tables" (v. 2). They were not putting down the task of waiting on tables, but simply saying that their gifts, as well as their calling, meant they needed to be involved in preaching, teaching and evangelizing. Is one gift "nobler" than other gifts? What Paul writes in 1 Corinthians 13 comes out of this question. In Corinth some people thought that speaking in tongues was the best spiritual gift of all. But Paul told them that LOVE was the greatest gift—and certainly serving food to needy widows is an act of love. A church that is to be unified and deal constructively with conflict must respect and use all kinds of gifts from all groups of people. The seven people chosen to do this task in today's passage are generally regarded as the first church deacons.

6:1 Many elderly Jews who had lived most of their lives elsewhere in the empire came to live in Jerusalem for their final years. Those who were widowed, now far from home, were subject to poverty. It was these women who were being neglected. In Old Testament as well as New Testament times, it was considered very important to take care of the needs of widows (Ex. 22:22–24; James 1:27). They had no "Social Security." Women didn't have access to most jobs. The church therefore acted to make sure that the needs of their widows were taken care of. **Grecian Jews.** These were Jews who came from outside Palestine and for whom Aramaic and Hebrew were relatively unknown languages. Their synagogue worship was also conducted in their native languages. *Hebraic Jews.* These were native Palestinians who spoke Aramaic as their daily language. Since all the apostles were Hebraic Jews, it may be that they were naturally more sensitive and aware of the needs of those with whom they could easily communicate. *being overlooked.* The word translated "being overlooked" might have meant that they received less food, or that they received less positive attention when the food was given out.

6:2 *wait on tables.* Literally, "to serve tables." This does not refer to being a waiter! Since people sitting at a table did banking at the time, to "serve tables" was a figure of speech for handling financial transactions. While many groups use this passage as the basis for the office of deacon, there is no title given to these men. However, the Greek verb "to serve" is the root word from which the English word "deacon" comes.

6:5 The names of the men chosen strongly indicate that all seven were Greek-speaking Jews. They perhaps also served as a bridge between the Palestinian apostles and the Greek-speaking Jews to help avoid further unintentional difficulties between the two groups. Some today might call it "trying to be politically correct." But they were not conscious of political correctness or incorrectness in this choice. Rather they were being conscious of the body of

Christ, and the need to keep it one. *Stephen.* This man moves to center stage in chapter 7, where he becomes the first Christian martyr. That he preached in this later story shows that he had gifts in addition to that of serving. *Philip.* Like Stephen, Philip demonstrated gifts of evangelism not unlike those of the apostles (8:4–8; 21:8). Of the other men nothing more is known.

6:6 *laid their hands on them.* In the Old Testament the laying on of hands signified either a blessing (Gen. 48:14) or a commissioning (Num. 27:18,23). It was a method by which the Holy Spirit was conveyed (13:2–3; 2 Tim. 1:6). It is most often done today with missionaries and newly ordained pastors, but may also be done with lay ministers. The Holy Spirit is the one who empowers the church, but also the one who binds us together as one. Divisive talk and action grieves the Holy Spirit (Eph. 4:29–32), and destroys the unity of the temple in which the Spirit lives (1 Cor. 3:16–17). Maintaining the unity of the church is hence not just an obligation to each other, but even more is an obligation to God.

6:7 *priests.* While the Sadducees controlled the priesthood, many of the priests, like Zechariah the father of John the Baptist (Luke 1:5), were sincerely devout men. Priests knew the most about sacrifice for sin, and the most spiritually sensitive among them no doubt understood that sacrificing an animal was inadequate. Only the sacrifice of the perfect Lamb of God could really atone for sin.

THE STONING OF STEPHEN

SCRIPTURE ACTS 6:8–15; 7:51–60

LAST WEEK

In last week's session we learned how the early church solved conflicts with the help of the Holy Spirit. We also were reminded about the importance of being sensitive to the needs of others and having the heart of a servant. Today we will learn more about Stephen, one of the seven chosen to serve in last week's Scripture passage. Stephen was the first Christian martyr and can teach us much about faith and forgiveness.

ICE-BREAKER   15 Min.
CONNECT WITH YOUR GROUP

LEADER

Introduce and welcome new group members. If there are no new members, choose one or two of the Ice-Breaker questions to get started. If there are new members, then discuss all three.

Encountering people who are opposed to your ideas and viewpoints can be a daily occurrence. Take turns sharing your experiences with dealing with "the opposition."

1. Who did you consider to be "the opposition" when you were in the seventh grade?
❏ Teachers.
❏ The opposite sex.
❏ Parents.
❏ A rival group in school.

2. When you were in the seventh grade, what was most likely to get your neighborhood "stirred up"?
❏ The crime problem.
❏ "Noisy kids," like you.
❏ Somebody who moved into the neighborhood whom people didn't like.
❏ Other _____.

3. What do you do right now that seems to get people "stirred up"?

BIBLE STUDY

READ SCRIPTURE AND DISCUSS

30 Min.

LEADER

Have two members of the group, selected ahead of time, read aloud the passage. Ask one member to read the part of Stephen, and the other to read the part of Luke, the narrator. The whole class should read the words of the false witnesses in verses 11 and 13–14.

The story of Stephen is one of the most inspiring in the history of the early church. We were introduced to Stephen in last week's Scripture. There he was described as "a man full of faith and of the Holy Spirit" (6:5). Read Acts 6:8–15; 7:51–60 and discover Stephen's unwavering, shining testimony as he faces extremely strong opposition.

The Stoning of Stephen

Luke: *8Now Stephen, a man full of God's grace and power, did great wonders and miraculous signs among the people. 9Opposition arose, however, from members of the Synagogue of the Freedmen (as it was called)—Jews of Cyrene and Alexandria as well as the provinces of Cilicia and Asia. These men began to argue with Stephen, 10but they could not stand up against his wisdom or the Spirit by whom he spoke. 11Then they secretly persuaded some men to say,*

Witnesses: *"We have heard Stephen speak words of blasphemy against Moses and against God."*

Luke: *12So they stirred up the people and the elders and the teachers of the law. They seized Stephen and brought him before the Sanhedrin. 13They produced false witnesses, who testified,*

Witnesses: *"This fellow never stops speaking against this holy place and against the law. 14For we have heard him say that this Jesus of Nazareth will destroy this place and change the customs Moses handed down to us."*

Luke: *15All who were sitting in the Sanhedrin looked intently at Stephen, and they saw that his face was like the face of an angel.*

Stephen: *51"You stiff-necked people, with uncircumcised hearts and ears! You are just like your fathers: You always resist the Holy Spirit! 52Was there ever a prophet your fathers did not persecute? They even killed those who predicted the coming of the Righteous One. And now you have betrayed and murdered him— 53you who have received the law that was put into effect through angels but have not obeyed it."*

Luke: *54When they heard this, they were furious and gnashed their teeth at him. 55But Stephen, full of the Holy Spirit, looked up to heaven and saw the glory of God, and Jesus standing at the right hand of God.*

Stephen:	*56 "Look," he said, "I see heaven open and the Son of Man standing at the right hand of God."*
Luke:	*57 At this they covered their ears and, yelling at the top of their voices, they all rushed at him, 58 dragged him out of the city and began to stone him. Meanwhile, the witnesses laid their clothes at the feet of a young man named Saul. 59 While they were stoning him, Stephen prayed,*
Stephen:	*"Lord Jesus, receive my spirit."*
Luke:	*60 Then he fell on his knees and cried out,*
Stephen:	*"Lord, do not hold this sin against them."*
Luke:	*When he had said this, he fell asleep.*

Acts 6:8–15; 7:51–60

QUESTIONS FOR INTERACTION

LEADER

Refer to the Summary and Study Notes at the end of this session as needed. If 30 minutes is not enough time to answer all of the questions in this section, conclude the Bible Study by answering question #7.

1. Had you been Stephen, what would you have done differently?
❒ Kept your mouth shut.
❒ Been more tactful.
❒ Gotten reinforcements from your "buds".
❒ Nothing.

2. What is Stephen doing that is getting the opposition group so upset? Are the issues listed in verses 13–14 the real issues, or are there other underlying issues?

3. What made Stephen's face appear like that of an angel?
❒ His relative innocence.
❒ The fact that God was speaking through him.
❒ He was getting ready to go to heaven.
❒ Other _____.

4. What is the significance of Stephen seeing Jesus ("the Son of Man") standing at the right hand of God (v. 56)?

5. What do Stephen's opponents do to indicate that they are no longer willing to listen?

6. Whose death does verse 60 remind you of?

7. What person who has injured you do you need to pray Stephen's prayer for, "Lord, do not hold this sin against them?"

GOING DEEPER: *If your group has time and/or wants a challenge, go on to this question.*

8. The people of Israel always seemed to revere the prophets of the past, but had trouble receiving prophets of the present (vv. 51–53). What makes it so hard to hear God's Word from someone in one's own time?

CARING TIME   15 Min.
APPLY THE LESSON AND PRAY FOR ONE ANOTHER

LEADER

Continue to encourage group members to invite new people to the group. Remind everyone that this group is for learning and sharing, but also for reaching out to others. Close the group prayer by thanking God for each member and for this time together.

Encourage and support one another in this time of prayer. Take turns sharing your responses to the following questions. Then share prayer requests and close with prayer.

1. Who or what is your biggest opposition to living the Christian life? How do you need God's help in overcoming this opposition?

2. What is something for which you are particularly thankful?

3. How has this group been an encouragement to you?

NEXT WEEK

Stephen's story has helped us to see that, with the help of the Holy Spirit, we can overcome any opposition we may face as we go on our journey through life. The power of God is stronger than any force we may encounter on this earth. In the coming week, pray for a missionary or someone you know who is being persecuted for their faith in Christ. Next week we will continue to see the miraculous power of God at work in Philip, as he obeys an angel of the Lord and shares his faith with an Ethiopian official.

Notes on Acts 6:8–15; 7:51–60

Summary: Ever since Jesus' death on a cross, thousands of his followers have followed in his footsteps to the point of being martyred themselves. These included persons like Paul who were beheaded, persons like Peter who were crucified (upside-down, in Peter's case), persons who were burned, stoned, drawn and quartered, fed to lions, and every other tortuous death imaginable. But in the midst of it all, the Christian faith has spread and prospered.

Stephen, whose death we read about in these passages, was the first in this long line. In a previous session we learned that Stephen was one of those selected to care for the widows of the Christian community. This would have necessitated gifts of service and caring. But apparently he also was not averse to preaching and evangelizing. The sermon he preached to the Sanhedrin was basically a summary of the Old Testament from the time of Abraham's call. The essence of his accusation against the Jewish religious leaders of his day was that they had never listened to God as he spoke through prophets down through history, and their rejection of Jesus was basically just one more chapter in that history. Certainly nothing in the sermon, as it is recorded for us, would justify the charge against Stephen that he blasphemed Moses or God (v. 11), or that he was seeking to change Jewish custom (v. 14). What seems to get these religious leaders angry is simply that Stephen was indicting them for failing to listen to and obey God's Word (vv. 53–54). Nothing gets a person angrier than having to hear a truth that they don't want to hear.

The Sanhedrin and Stephen's other opponents reacted to Stephen's sermon by deciding to stop listening. They showed this in two ways. They covered their ears, and they started yelling at the "top of their voices" (v. 57). As anyone who has ever gotten involved in a "family discussion" knows, yelling is perhaps the best way to show you are no longer truly listening to what the other person is saying. Why did they stop listening? Stephen would have said that they were once again "resisting the Holy Spirit" (v. 51). Another possibility is that what they had heard to that point was too painfully close to the truth for them to listen anymore. They were becoming hardened.

The good news for the Christian church, however, was that not all of those present completely hardened themselves on that day. One young man named Saul was resisting at that point and cooperating in the stoning, but eventually his heart would be turned by a vision on the road to Damascus; and he would be called Paul, the most influential of all Christian evangelists. Perhaps he listened to more from Stephen than he had let on, and what he heard may have prepared him for that Damascus road experience. In any case, the closed ears and angry yelling did not thwart the work of the Holy Spirit—it was just redirected.

6:9 *Synagogue of the Freedmen.* The Freedmen were former Roman slaves (or their descendants) released by their masters and granted Roman citizenship. The Greek-speaking Jews who left home and family to settle in Jerusalem were especially devoted to the temple and its religious system.

6:10–13 From the charges in verses 13–14, it appears that the opponents of Stephen felt his message about Jesus threatened the sanctity of the Law of Moses and the sacrificial system of the temple. Unable to out-argue Stephen (v. 10), they resorted to trumped-up charges of blasphemy (v. 11) so that he could be tried before the San-hedrin.

6:14 The root of the complaint against Stephen was the charge that the followers of Jesus threatened to destroy the temple and replace the laws of Moses with their own ways. The fact is that Stephen, follow-ing Jesus, probably did preach something that could have been misconstrued in this way. Jesus spoke of destroying the temple in a way that was likewise misunderstood (Mark 14:58; John 2:19–22). Stephen taught that since Jesus himself was the new "place" of worship where the presence of God could truly be known, the temple was no longer necessary since Jesus offered the final, ultimate sacrifice (Heb. 9–10). Jesus also spoke of the destruction of the temple that was to come (Luke 21:5–6); Stephen, in repeating this warning of judgment that would result if the Jews rejected Jesus as their Messiah, may have been misunderstood as inferring that the Christians were plotting an all out attack on the temple. Regarding the second charge, Jesus repeatedly challenged the oral tradi-tions that had developed around the Law (Matt. 5:21–48; 9:14–15; 12:2ff). As far as the Jewish leaders were concerned, to challenge this tradition was to challenge the Law itself. If Stephen followed Jesus' lead in this matter, then he too would be seen as one who was advocating carelessness about the Law.

6:15 *like the face of an angel.* Ironically, the only other biblical character who shared this experience was Moses whom Stephen was charged with defying (Ex. 34:29–31; 2 Cor. 3:13)!

7:51 *stiff-necked people.* The image is that of a people refusing to bow their head

before God (Ex. 33:5; Deut. 10:16). *uncir-cumcised hearts and ears.* Physical cir-cumcision was always intended as a symbol of a heart set apart for God and ears open to do his will.

7:52 Jewish tradition held that Isaiah was sawn in two by the evil king Manasseh and that Jews in Egypt stoned Jeremiah. Jesus also warned the leaders that in rejecting him they were following in the same foot-steps as their fathers (Luke 11:47–51).

7:53 The final accusation Stephen makes is that these leaders are the ones who violate Moses' law. *through angels.* Jewish (and Christian) tradition taught the Law was given through the mediation of angels (Gal. 3:19; Heb 2:2), whereas the Gospel is announced directly by the Messiah himself.

7:56 *the Son of Man.* This was the title that Jesus most frequently used for himself, and it is particularly significant that he used this image to describe himself at his trial before this same Sanhedrin (Dan. 7:13; Mark 14:62). The fact that Jesus, as the Son of Man, is at the right hand of God means that the way is open for all people everywhere to come to God.

7:58 John 18:31 indicates the Sanhedrin did not have the legal right of capital pun-ishment, so this may be an act of mob vio-lence. However, Acts 26:10 indicates that perhaps by this time Pilate's ability to con-trol the Sanhedrin had drastically weak-ened and it indeed took capital cases into its own hands. *Saul.* This is the one who was to become the great apostle.

7:59–60 See Luke 23:34,46.

PHILIP AND THE ETHIOPIAN

SCRIPTURE ACTS 8:26–40

LAST WEEK

We were inspired last week by the story of Stephen, the first martyr for the Christian faith. Stephen reminded us to keep our eyes on Jesus and never resist the guidance of the Holy Spirit. Today Philip, another gifted disciple, shows us how to share our faith effectively.

ICE-BREAKER
CONNECT WITH YOUR GROUP

15 Min.

LEADER

Choose one, two or all three of the Ice-Breaker questions. Be sure to welcome and introduce new group members.

We all need a little help now and then, and how we appreciate it when someone takes the time to give us that help. Take turns sharing your experiences with needing or receiving help.

1. Did you find yourself hitchhiking when you were in college or when your car broke down? What kind of person(s) did you meet at this time?

2. What do you read that you are the most likely to need help in understanding?
    ❏ Government forms.
    ❏ The Bible.
    ❏ Your insurance policy.
    ❏ Your children's homework.
    ❏ Other _____.

3. When you don't understand something, what are you most likely to do?

❏ Act like you do understand.

❏ Ask questions.

❏ Get angry at whoever wrote or said it.

❏ Other _____.

BIBLE STUDY

READ SCRIPTURE AND DISCUSS

30 Min.

LEADER

Select a member of the group ahead of time to read aloud the passage. Then discuss the Questions for Interaction, dividing into subgroups of four or five.

Philip was a disciple that had a gift for helping others. He was chosen as one of the seven to serve and help the widows, as we studied in Session 6. He had a very successful ministry in Samaria (8:4–8), and his miracles there caused "great joy." In today's Scripture, Philip is called to help a foreigner understand the Word of God. Read Acts 8:26–40 and see how gently and effectively Philip leads this man to Christ.

Philip and the Ethiopian Eunuch

²⁶ Now an angel of the Lord said to Philip, "Go south to the road— the desert road—that goes down from Jerusalem to Gaza." ²⁷ So he started out, and on his way he met an Ethiopian eunuch, an important official in charge of all the treasury of Candace, queen of the Ethiopians. This man had gone to Jerusalem to worship, ²⁸ and on his way home was sitting in his chariot reading the book of Isaiah the prophet. ²⁹ The Spirit told Philip, "Go to that chariot and stay near it."

³⁰ Then Philip ran up to the chariot and heard the man reading Isaiah the prophet. "Do you understand what you are reading?" Philip asked.

³¹ "How can I," he said, "unless someone explains it to me?" So he invited Philip to come up and sit with him. ³² The eunuch was reading this passage of Scripture:

"He was led like a sheep to the slaughter,
and as a lamb before the shearer is silent,
so he did not open his mouth.
³³ In his humiliation he was deprived of justice.
Who can speak of his descendants?
For his life was taken from the earth."

³⁴ The eunuch asked Philip, "Tell me, please, who is the prophet talking about, himself or someone else?" ³⁵ Then Philip began with that very passage of Scripture and told him the good news about Jesus.

36As they traveled along the road, they came to some water and the eunuch said, "Look, here is water. Why shouldn't I be baptized?" 38And he gave orders to stop the chariot. Then both Philip and the eunuch went down into the water and Philip baptized him. 39When they came up out of the water, the Spirit of the Lord suddenly took Philip away, and the eunuch did not see him again, but went on his way rejoicing. 40Philip, however, appeared at Azotus and traveled about, preaching the gospel in all the towns until he reached Caesarea.

Acts 8:26–40

QUESTIONS FOR INTERACTION

LEADER

Refer to the Summary and Study Notes at the end of this session as needed. If 30 minutes is not enough time to answer all of the questions in this section, conclude the Bible Study by answering question #7.

1. What are you most likely to be doing when you are returning from worship?
   ❏ Thinking about the sermon.
   ❏ Venting your anger about something you didn't like in the service.
   ❏ Arguing with the family.
   ❏ Just listening to the radio.
   ❏ Thinking about dinner.
   ❏ Other _____.

2. What would you say was the most important key to Philip's success in sharing his faith in this story.
   ❏ His following of the Spirit's lead.
   ❏ His sensitivity to the eunuch's need.
   ❏ His knowledge of Scripture.
   ❏ Other _____.

3. What passage of Scripture was the eunuch reading? Where can it be found? Why was it a particularly relevant passage for Philip to share what Jesus had done?

4. What questions did the eunuch ask that opened the way to Philip's sharing? What do these questions show about the eunuch?

5. How does the eunuch's mood at the beginning of the story differ from his mood at the end (v. 39)? How do you think this mood change affected the people who knew him when he returned to work for Candace?

6. In your spiritual journey, what "Philip" has come alongside you and helped you find direction?

7. What spiritual question or struggle could you use a "Philip" to help you figure out right now?

GOING DEEPER: *If your group has time and/or wants a challenge, go on to this question.*

8. How can a person determine when the Holy Spirit is leading him or her to do something (like talking to this eunuch), and when it's just his or her own impulses?

CARING TIME   15 Min.

APPLY THE LESSON AND PRAY FOR ONE ANOTHER

LEADER

Have you started working with your group about their mission—perhaps by sharing the dream of multiplying into two groups by the end of this study of Acts?

Praying for one another is a great help in time of need or concern. Take time now to share your responses to the questions below. Then share prayer requests and close with a time of prayer.

1. In what area of your life do you need some help? How difficult is it for you to ask for help?

2. How do you feel about sharing the Good News of Jesus with others? What do you need most from the Holy Spirit to help you with taking that risk?

3. Who is someone you could invite to join this group?

NEXT WEEK

Today's story about Philip and the Ethiopian has been a wonderful example of how much we can be a help to others if we are open to God's leading. We also saw how God brought help to the Ethiopian when he needed it, so we can be assured that God will do the same for us if we are willing to recognize and accept that help. In the coming week, pray to be open to the leading of the Holy Spirit. Next week we will see how God can change any person's heart, no matter how evil that person may seem. We will be studying the conversion of Saul, a murderer of the Christians, to Paul, a great evangelist to the Gentiles.

NOTES ON ACTS 8:26–40

· ·

Summary: While the evangelistic methods of the early church included sermons with mass conversions, as in Acts 2:14–41, one-on-one sharing was also important. Nowhere do we see that more clearly than in this story about Philip and the Ethiopian. Philip shows this low-key style in his interaction with the Ethiopian eunuch. This eunuch had come a long way to worship in Jerusalem, in spite of the fact that as a eunuch he could not fully participate in the temple worship. That showed a real spiritual hunger! His hunger becomes even more evident when we see him still studying the Scripture on his way home from worshiping in Jerusalem. Philip let this need guide their interaction. He didn't just barge in and force his "spiritual wisdom" on the man. He asked whether or not the eunuch needed help with the Scripture he was examining. Then, even after the man said that he did, he waited for the eunuch to invite him in (v. 31). Philip was not a "stick your foot in the door" kind of guy. He then responded to questions like the one in verse 34 and, when it was all over, it was the eunuch himself who brought up the idea of baptism (v. 37). Certainly not all person-to-person evangelism flows along with this kind of ease, or these kinds of quick results. But Philip's method sets a good example.

8:26 *an angel of the Lord.* A Jewish expression for the Spirit of God (see vv. 29,39). **the road.** Two roads, one of which went through a desert area, led from Jerusalem to the old city of Gaza.

8:27 *eunuch.* Eunuchs were commonly employed as royal officials. Although attracted to Judaism, as a eunuch he would never be allowed to fully participate in the temple worship (Deut. 23:1). **Candace.** A dynastic title for the Ethiopian queens.

8:28 *chariot.* While we have visions of light war chariots racing along behind fleet Arabian horses, it is probable that the eunuch was in a slow-moving, ox-drawn cart accompanied by a retinue of servants.

8:32–33 The eunuch was reading from Isaiah 53:7–8, a key Old Testament passage about the Servant of the Lord. This particular passage underlines much of what Luke has already recorded about the apostles' preaching concerning the identity of Jesus (3:13; 4:27).

8:34 *who is the prophet talking about?* The eunuch's question was a common one in Jewish circles. Some thought the prophet was speaking of his own sufferings as one rejected, while others thought he was speaking figuratively of Israel as a nation that suffered at the hands of its oppressors (Isa. 44:1–2). Still another view of the Servant's identity linked him with Cyrus the King of Persia (Isa. 44:28–45:3). The traditional rabbis had not made any connection between the Suffering Servant of Isaiah 53, the kingly Messiah of Isaiah 11, and the glorified Son of Man in Daniel 7:13. Only in Jesus' teachings did these concepts come together (Luke 24:26).

8:35 Philip used this passage as a jumping off point to explain the ministry of Jesus. He undoubtedly referred the eunuch to other verses in Isaiah 53, as well as to the other references about the Servant in Isaiah that point out the Servant's suffering for the sake of others and how this Servant would be a light for the Gentiles. All of this would have been related to Jesus' ministry, death and resurrection. To the age-old question of why God allows the good to suffer, the Christian answer would become—God himself suffered in the person of his Son. ***Philip began.*** Literally, "opened up his mouth." The same word is used in Acts 10:34; it connotes a solemn pronouncement. ***the good news.*** This *Gospel* is not gloom and doom, but a message of joy—God came in Christ to take on and defeat suffering and death.

8:36–38 *Why shouldn't I.* The Greek word behind this expression also occurs in the baptismal accounts of Cornelius in Acts 10:47 and 11:17. It may be part of a baptismal liturgy the early church used with candidates for baptism. The strict Jew would offer at least one reason why he was ineligible to be considered part of God's people: he was a eunuch. Although due to his castration this man could never become a Jewish proselyte (see note on v. 27), he was able to become a full member of the church through Jesus Christ. This fulfills the prophecy of Isaiah 56:3–8, which anticipates a time when both foreigners *and* eunuchs would be welcomed into God's household. Luke may have included this particular story to illustrate just that truth. Verse 37 is an addition not found in the earliest manuscripts. A Christian scribe who wished to highlight what was required of a candidate for Christian baptism apparently added it at a later date.

8:39 Another ancient text has an additional phrase here. Keeping in mind that in Greek adjectives commonly follow the noun that they modify, this longer account (with the additional words italicized) is literally translated, "the Spirit *Holy fell upon the eunuch but the angel* of the Lord suddenly took Philip away." While it does not change the meaning of the passage at all, it can be seen how a copyist may have inadvertently dropped out this phrase, which completes the story better, at a later date. ***took Philip away.*** Whether this was a miraculous act of God (1 Kings 18:12) or another way of describing a command of the Spirit to Philip (v. 26) is uncertain. ***rejoicing.*** The joy of the eunuch reflects that of the believers in Jerusalem (2:46) and Samaria (8:8), another evidence of the Spirit.

8:40 *Azotus.* Another city on the coast of the Mediterranean Sea about 20 miles north of Gaza. ***Caesarea.*** The Roman seat of power in Judea, about 60 miles up the coast from Azotus. Philip evangelized throughout the Jewish communities along the Palestinian coast of the Mediterranean.

SESSION 9
PAUL'S CONVERSION

SCRIPTURE   ACTS 9:1–19

LAST WEEK

In last week's session we saw how Philip was led by the Holy Spirit to share the Good News of Jesus with a foreigner, an Ethiopian official. As a result, the Ethiopian was converted to Christianity and baptized on the spot! Today we will witness another conversion. A conversion that is so intense and supernatural it changes a murderer of Christians into one of the most zealous apostles that has ever lived.

ICE-BREAKER   15 Min.
CONNECT WITH YOUR GROUP

LEADER

Welcome and introduce new group members. Choose one, two or all three Ice-Breaker questions, depending on your group's needs.

Some days are better than others! Take turns sharing some of the ups and downs you've encountered on your journey through life.

1. When you were in grade school, were you most likely to be "the persecuted" or "the persecutor" in relation to the other kids in the school? How did you deal with it when you were given a hard time?

2. How would you describe the "road" that you are on at this point in your life?
   ❒ Rough and rocky.
   ❒ Steep and exhausting.
   ❒ Smooth and easy.
   ❒ All uphill.
   ❒ Other _____.

3. If you had to do without one of your senses for a period of time, which sense would you choose?

BIBLE STUDY

READ SCRIPTURE AND DISCUSS

30 Min.

LEADER

Ask four group members, selected ahead of time, to read aloud the passage. Have one member read Luke's narration; another read the part of the Lord; another read the part of Saul; and the fourth person read the part of Ananias.

In Session 7, we studied the stoning of Stephen, a wonderful disciple filled with the Holy Spirit. The verse following that section read, "And Saul was there, giving approval to his death" (8:1). It is this man's conversion that we will be learning about in the Scripture for today. Read Acts 9:1–19 and see how God has the power to change any person's heart.

Paul's Conversion

Luke: **9** *Meanwhile, Saul was still breathing out murderous threats against the Lord's disciples. He went to the high priest ²and asked him for letters to the synagogues in Damascus, so that if he found any there who belonged to the Way, whether men or women, he might take them as prisoners to Jerusalem. ³As he neared Damascus on his journey, suddenly a light from heaven flashed around him. ⁴He fell to the ground and heard a voice say to him,*

The Lord: *"Saul, Saul, why do you persecute me?"*

Saul: *⁵"Who are you, Lord?" Saul asked.*

The Lord: *"I am Jesus, whom you are persecuting," he replied. ⁶"Now get up and go into the city, and you will be told what you must do."*

Luke: *⁷The men traveling with Saul stood there speechless; they heard the sound but did not see anyone. ⁸Saul got up from the ground, but when he opened his eyes he could see nothing. So they led him by the hand into Damascus. ⁹For three days he was blind, and did not eat or drink anything. ¹⁰In Damascus there was a disciple named Ananias. The Lord called to him in a vision,*

The Lord: *"Ananias!"*

Ananias: *"Yes, Lord," he answered.*

The Lord: *¹¹The Lord told him, "Go to the house of Judas on Straight Street and ask for a man from Tarsus named Saul, for he is praying. ¹²In a vision he has seen a man named Ananias come and place his hands on him to restore his sight."*

Ananias: *¹³"Lord," Ananias answered, "I have heard many reports about this man and all the harm he has done to your saints in Jerusalem. ¹⁴And he has* come here with authority from the chief priests to arrest all who call on your name."

The Lord: *[15]But the Lord said to Ananias, "Go! This man is my chosen instrument to carry my name before the Gentiles and their kings and before the people of Israel. [16]I will show him how much he must suffer for my name."*

Luke: *[17]Then Ananias went to the house and entered it. Placing his hands on Saul, he said,*

Ananias: *"Brother Saul, the Lord—Jesus, who appeared to you on the road as you were coming here—has sent me so that you may see again and be filled with the Holy Spirit."*

Luke: *[18]Immediately, something like scales fell from Saul's eyes, and he could see again. He got up and was baptized, [19]and after taking some food, he regained his strength.*

Acts 9:1–19

LEADER

Refer to the Summary and Study Notes at the conclusion of this session as needed. If 30 minutes is not enough time to answer all of the questions in this section, conclude the Bible Study by answering question #8.

QUESTIONS FOR INTERACTION

1. If Christ were to meet you on the road to call you on the carpet for something you used to do in your younger years, what would it be?

2. What do you believe motivated Saul in his zeal for persecuting Christians?
   ❐ A sincere desire to do what was right.
   ❐ A need to quiet his own doubts by attacking divergent opinions.
   ❐ A desire to win points with God.
   ❐ Other _____.

3. What gave Saul the power to change?

4. What do you think was the significance of the fact that the other men with Saul did not see anyone?

5. Why do you think God struck Saul with blindness as part of this vision?

6. Had you been Ananias and God called on you to go minister to Saul, how would you have responded?

7. In your own coming to Christ, who was the Ananias God used to help turn you around?

8. Who might God be calling you to be an "Ananias" for right now?

GOING DEEPER: *If your group has time and/or wants a challenge, go on to this question.*

9. Based on his past behavior, Saul was a dangerous person to Ananias. How can you tell when it is okay to take a risk on a dangerous person being able to change?

CARING TIME   15 Min.
APPLY THE LESSON AND PRAY FOR ONE ANOTHER

LEADER

Have you identified someone in the group that could be a leader for a new small group when your group divides? How could you encourage and mentor that person?

Use this time to pray for one another, and for your own special concerns. Take turns sharing responses to the following questions. Then close with a time of group prayer, asking God to give you the strength to keep praying for those you've almost given up on.

1. Rate this past week on a scale of 1 (terrible) to 10 (great). What's the outlook for this week?

2. Who have you been praying many years for, but that person still hasn't become a Christian? How can you help this person?

3. In what area of your life would you like to see more change?

NEXT WEEK

Today's story about Paul's conversion is one we can turn to again and again for encouragement. If God can change a persecutor of Christians into a great evangelist, we know he can change our family members and friends who refuse to accept Jesus as their Savior. In the coming week, take some extra time to pray for the conversion of those you know who are resisting the call to become a Christian. Next week we will consider a conversion of a different kind when Peter begins to accept that the Gentiles are also included in God's salvation plan.

NOTES ON ACTS 9:1–19

Summary: One thing the Bible doesn't ever seem to do is look at its central characters through rose-colored glasses and try to make them out to be overly perfect heroes. Moses murdered a man. David had an affair with Bathsheba, and tried to cover it up by a murder. Peter denied his Lord. And now in Acts we read the story of Saul, who later became Paul, the Christian church's greatest evangelist. When we first hear of him, he is a persecutor of the church, cooperating with a lynch mob (8:1)! And now, in this passage, he is taking a more active role in seeking to imprison and even kill Christians. That the Bible is so honest about its heroes should help us to trust it even more.

Saul's vision on the road to Damascus is one of the most profound conversion stories in history. As Paul, he later referred to it no less than four times to validate his authority as an apostle (1 Cor. 9:1; 15:8; 2 Cor. 4:6; Gal. 1:15–16). Saul later equated his vision of the risen Lord with those who saw Jesus in the flesh before his death and resurrection. Such a direct, face-to-face experience with Jesus was needed to have the status of an apostle.

Paul's witness after this event was particularly powerful due to the radical change in his life. It was so powerful that the Jewish traditionalists wasted no time in trying to kill him (9:23). (The text in verse 23 says "the Jews," but remember Paul and many other Christians were Jews as well. In Acts, the term "the Jews" refers to the traditional Jewish leadership.) In a similar way, the Jewish religious leadership in Jerusalem sought to kill Lazarus after he had been raised from the dead, so powerful was his testimony (John 12:10). To save Saul, the other disciples of Damascus had to go out at night to lower him in a basket through an opening in the wall (9:25). It would not be the last time that Saul would be in danger because of his boldness in proclaiming the Gospel of Christ. His life change had taken him from being the hunter to being the hunted. But it was a life change that he would have said made it all worth it!

9:1 *breathing out murderous threats.* This reflects the depth of Saul's obsessive hatred toward the Christians. After hearing Stephen's speech (7:1–53), he undoubtedly viewed the Christians as an anti-establishment, heretical sect determined to undermine the Law of God and the worship of the temple. His ability to carry out his threats of murder would certainly have been proscribed by Roman law, but apparently he and the Sanhedrin had some success in their program (26:10).

9:2 *letters.* While the Sanhedrin had no formal authority outside of Judea, its prestige could influence elders in synagogues far from Jerusalem. In this case, the Sanhedrin asked the elders in Damascus to cooperate with Saul by allowing him to arrest as blasphemers those Christians who had fled from Jerusalem to Damascus and bring them for trial in Jerusalem. The book of Maccabees speaks of the Sanhedrin requesting officials in Egypt to give them extradition rights over Palestinian lawbreakers who had fled there. ***Damascus.*** A city about 150 miles from Jerusalem. Luke has not told us how the church began among the sizable Jewish community in this important city, but Saul desired to expand his persecution there so that it might not spread any further. This incident reveals how central Saul was to the carrying out of this first wave of persecution: once he was converted, this persecution dissipated (9:31). ***the Way.*** This phrase is unique to Acts as a name for Christianity (19:9,23; 22:4; 24:14,22). It may stem from Jesus' claim in John 14:6. It was not until later at Antioch that they were first called "Christians." In any case, even then they were seen not as a distinctly new religion, but as a group within Judaism.

9:3 *a light from heaven flashed around him.* The term is often used of lightning, indicating the brilliance of the light (26:13). Light (glory) is commonly connected with divine appearances (Luke 9:29; Rev. 1:14–16).

9:4 *why do you persecute me.* The opposition Saul created for the church was really directed against its head, Jesus, demonstrating the identity between Jesus and the church, his body (Luke 10:16). God is bringing Saul face-to-face with the fact that by his activities he is not honoring God, but resisting the One glorified by God.

9:9 This profound experience shattered all of Saul's previous convictions. Humbled and blinded, he fasted as he awaited what Jesus would do next with him.

9:10 Apart from Paul's comment in Acts 22:12, nothing is known of Ananias.

9:11–12 The vision Ananias received was matched by one Saul had of his coming. This double-dream confirmation is also seen in the story of Peter and Cornelius (ch. 10).

9:11 *Straight Street.* This street is still one of the main thoroughfares of Damascus. Nothing is known of Judas.

9:13 *Lord.* This title for Jesus, highlighting his authority, is a common one in this account (9:5,11,13,15,17); and in Paul's writings. *saints.* Literally, "holy ones." This was a common term for Israel in the Old Testament. Ananias applies it to Christians, as does Paul in his letters. It means those people who are separated out for God.

9:14 *all who call on your name.* This way of referring to Christians comes from Joel 2:32. In the book of Joel it was God's name (Yahweh) that was to be called upon: the fact that the early Christians transferred this to Jesus is a clear indication of their belief in his divinity.

9:15–16 The Lord overruled Ananias with a final command to "Go!" and a description of what Saul's mission would be.

9:15 *my chosen instrument.* Literally, "a choice vessel." Some images for the Old Testament form the context here. Israel was compared to a vessel in the hand of a potter, formed to perform the task for which the potter created it (Jer. 18:1–6). The Servant of Isaiah was God's chosen (Isa. 44:1): Saul (soon to be Paul) would carry on the mission of the Servant in terms of bringing the light to the Gentiles (Isa. 42:6; 49:6) *and* in sharing in his suffering.

9:17 *Placing his hands on Saul.* Laying on of hands was a common way of conveying the Holy Spirit (8:17–18; 13:3; 19:6). *Brother Saul.* Without further question, Ananias affirms Saul as part of the family through the grace of Jesus. After laying hands on him, Saul's sight was restored; he was baptized (presumably by Ananias); and was filled with the Holy Spirit. Even with this healing, however, there are indications that Paul may have had continued problems with his sight. He had someone else actually pen his letters (Rom. 16:22), and when he did write with his own hand, he noted how big the letters were (Gal. 6:11). This might indicate a continuing sight problem.

SESSION 10
PETER'S VISION

SCRIPTURE   ACTS 10:1–23

LAST WEEK

Paul's conversion from a persecutor of Christians to a zealous apostle was the inspirational story we studied in last week's session. We were reminded that with God nothing is impossible and any person can be changed. This week we will see how God changes Peter's heart to accept the Gentiles in God's plan of salvation.

ICE-BREAKER   15 Min.
CONNECT WITH YOUR GROUP

LEADER

Choose one or two of the Ice-Breaker questions. If you have a new group member you may want to do all three. Remember to stick closely to the three-part agenda and the time allowed for each segment.

Adapting to change and new ideas is something life often brings our way. Take turns sharing about times you've been challenged with trying new foods or dreaming new dreams.

1. What kind of food are you most hesitant to eat when it is set before you? If it is served at a place where you are a guest, do you politely eat it anyway or speak up?

2. What is the most unusual food you have ever been asked to eat?

3. What is the most interesting dream that you remember having recently? Are your dreams ever repeated? Do they have sequels?

BIBLE STUDY

READ SCRIPTURE AND DISCUSS

30 Min.

LEADER

Select a member of the group ahead of time to read the passage. Then discuss the Questions for Interaction, dividing into subgroups of four or five.

At the time of the early church there were many barriers and divisions between the Jews and the Gentiles. Peter was a very devout Jew, along with now being a Christian. Read Acts 10:1–23 and see how God teaches Peter that these barriers should no longer exist and salvation is for all people.

Peter's Vision

10 *At Caesarea there was a man named Cornelius, a centurion in what was known as the Italian Regiment. ²He and all his family were devout and God-fearing; he gave generously to those in need and prayed to God regularly. ³One day at about three in the afternoon he had a vision. He distinctly saw an angel of God, who came to him and said, "Cornelius!"*

⁴Cornelius stared at him in fear. "What is it, Lord?" he asked.

The angel answered, "Your prayers and gifts to the poor have come up as a memorial offering before God. ⁵Now send men to Joppa to bring back a man named Simon who is called Peter. ⁶He is staying with Simon the tanner, whose house is by the sea."

⁷When the angel who spoke to him had gone, Cornelius called two of his servants and a devout soldier who was one of his attendants. ⁸He told them everything that had happened and sent them to Joppa.

⁹About noon the following day as they were on their journey and approaching the city, Peter went up on the roof to pray. ¹⁰He became hungry and wanted something to eat, and while the meal was being prepared, he fell into a trance. ¹¹He saw heaven opened and something like a large sheet being let down to earth by its four corners. ¹²It contained all kinds of four-footed animals, as well as reptiles of the earth and birds of the air. ¹³Then a voice told him, "Get up, Peter. Kill and eat."

¹⁴"Surely not, Lord!" Peter replied. "I have never eaten anything impure or unclean."

¹⁵The voice spoke to him a second time, "Do not call anything impure that God has made clean."

¹⁶This happened three times, and immediately the sheet was taken back to heaven.

¹⁷While Peter was wondering about the meaning of the vision, the men sent by Cornelius found out where Simon's house was and stopped at the gate. ¹⁸They called out, asking if Simon who was known as Peter was staying there.

¹⁹While Peter was still thinking about the vision, the Spirit said to him, "Simon, three men are looking for you. ²⁰So get up and go downstairs. Do not hesitate to go with them, for I have sent them."

²¹Peter went down and said to the men, "I'm the one you're looking for. Why have you come?"

²²The men replied, "We have come from Cornelius the centurion. He is a righteous and God-fearing man, who is respected by all the Jewish people. A holy angel told him to have you come to his house so that he could hear what you have to say." ²³Then Peter invited the men into the house to be his guests.

Acts 10:1–23

LEADER

Refer to the Summary and Study Notes at the conclusion of this session as needed. If 30 minutes is not enough time to answer all of the questions in this section, conclude the Bible Study by answering question #8.

QUESTIONS FOR INTERACTION

1. When have you, like Peter, had a dream through which you suspected God might be trying to tell you something?

2. What impresses you most about Cornelius?

3. Had you been Peter, what would have been going through your mind when you saw the vision of the animals in the sheet?

4. Why did Peter hesitate to follow the directions of the voice in his vision?

5. Why would Jews like Peter have especially hated Cornelius?

6. Are there persons or groups who, if God wanted you to socialize with and witness to them, he would have to first open your heart to them in a vision or dream? Which person or groups might they be?

7. What is the central learning Peter had from this vision?

8. How would it change your behavior if you truly believed that no classification or group of persons was "unclean"?

GOING DEEPER: *If your group has time and/or wants a challenge, go on to this question.*

9. Have you ever come to the conclusion that a rule of behavior you were raised with no longer applies? How do you know when it is truly God who is leading you to such a new perspective?

CARING TIME   15 Min.

APPLY THE LESSON AND PRAY FOR ONE ANOTHER

LEADER

Conclude the group prayer time today by reading Galatians 3:28: *There is neither Jew nor Greek, slave nor free, male nor female, for you are all one in Christ Jesus.*

Begin this Caring Time by sharing your responses to the following questions. Then take some time to share prayer requests and pray for one another.

1. If this past week were a meal, what kind of meal would it have been?
    ❏ Hamburger and French fries.
    ❏ A thick, juicy steak.
    ❏ Gourmet cuisine.
    ❏ Burnt pot roast.
    ❏ Bread and water.
    ❏ Other _____.

    What seems to be on the menu for next week?

2. What type of person would you find difficult to invite to this group or your church? How do you need God to change your heart?

3. If God were to visit you in a vision, what is the first question you would ask him?

NEXT WEEK

Today we saw how God was at work in Peter's life, helping him to understand that salvation was truly meant for all people, not just the Jews. What matters is the attitude of a person's heart, and not the rules they may or may not follow. This was a truly different way of thinking for any devout Jew. In the coming week, reach out to someone who is of a different culture or religion and pray for that person. Next week we will study how this change in perspective is passed on to Barnabas, Saul (soon to be called Paul) and other believers, resulting in the growth of the church in Antioch.

Notes on Acts 10:1–23

Summary: Perhaps the biggest cultural division of biblical times was the division between Jew and Gentile. It would have been comparable to the division between black and white, Arab and Jew, or Japanese and Korean in our modern society. To understand what God did to heal this division in the church, we first need to understand how it developed.

God had called the Jews to be distinct from the people around them, and part of this distinction included what they would eat. Peter was a good Jew and followed Old Testament dietary laws (Lev.11:1–47). The importance of many of these laws may seem to elude us today, but they were probably grounded in health issues. They were also part of what separated Jews from the people around them. Such a separation was needed so that Jews wouldn't just blend into other cultures, all of which worshiped other gods, and some of which practiced the especially abominable practices of child sacrifice and cult prostitution. God wanted them to see themselves as different from the people who did such practices. However, there is sometimes a fine line between hating the behavior of a people and hating the people, and over time many Jews came to hate all Gentiles.

It was in this context that the story about Peter occurs. It helps us to understand that when this event happened in the life of Peter, God wasn't just changing a dietary law. Rather, he was announcing a change in the way Jews were to look at the people of the cultures around them. When Peter hesitated to follow the instruction of the voice that told him to eat the "unclean" food, he was told, "Do not call anything impure that God has made clean" (v. 15). The voice convinced Peter and he had a new insight about human relationships. When he later went to Cornelius, he shared what he had learned; "... God has shown me that I should not call any man impure or unclean" (10:28). This insight opened the way for a church that became multicultural, as men and women from many nations joined together in one faith.

10:1 *Cornelius.* Romans typically used three names. Cornelius, a popular name taken on by the descendants of slaves who were released from slavery by the action of a P. Cornelius Sculla in 82 B.C., would have been this soldier's middle name. ***a centurion.*** Equivalent to the rank of an army captain in today's terms. As such he was a representative of the military oppression of Rome, a hated foreign culture. ***the Italian Regiment.*** An auxiliary force stationed in the area composed of men recruited from Italy.

10:2 *God-fearing.* The distinction between Gentile God-fearers (who believed in the true God and obeyed his ethical commands) and proselytes (who fully converted to Judaism) lay in the hesitancy of the former to submit to the Jewish ceremonial laws, especially circumcision. Cornelius demonstrated his faith by practicing the Jewish disciplines of prayer and almsgiving. He "gave generously to those in need" and "prayed to God regularly." Thus he loved God and neighbor, as the two greatest commandments called him to do.

10:3 *about three in the afternoon.* This was the time for afternoon prayers at the temple in Jerusalem. Although Cornelius would never be able to participate fully in the temple services, he may have followed its pattern in terms of his own mode and time for prayer.

10:4 *Lord.* Cornelius did not yet know of Jesus, so this is an expression of respect for what Cornelius recognized as a divine visitor. *as a memorial offering to God.* Although Cornelius would not have been allowed to offer animal sacrifices in the temple, the angel lets him know that his heart-attitude of devotion to God is recognized as a real sacrifice that is acceptable to God.

10:5–8 Told by the angel to send for Peter in Joppa, Cornelius sends three men to do so, at least one of whom shared his devotion to God.

10:9 *about noon.* When apart from the temple, many devout Jews prayed at 9 A.M., noon, and 3 P.M. (Ps. 55:17). *up on the roof.* Roofs were flat and often used as places for people to sit or sleep.

10:12 *all kinds of four-footed animals.* These animals included those that the law had proscribed as food.

10:14 *Lord.* Typically in Acts, this word is used as a title for Jesus. Peter may have recognized his dream as coming from the Lord, but he was not willing to simply follow the Lord's invitation to eat of the food.

10:15 In Mark 7:19 Jesus laid the groundwork for the pronouncement that, despite the laws of Leviticus 11, food simply was not a spiritual issue. Such laws had their place earlier in Jewish history as a means of separating them from the pagans in neighboring areas, and as an object lesson about the meaning of holiness (that is, being separated out for God's use). (For an Old Testament story where eating became an issue for young Jewish men who sought to retain their cultural identity, read Dan.1:3–17.) However, Jesus' point was to show that these object lessons were not to be mistaken as God's ultimate concern: his interest was in genuine, inward holiness that had nothing to do with external matters such as food, circumcision, etc. Demonstrating the reality of this

was the burden of much of Paul's ministry (Rom. 2:25–29; 14:13–18; 1 Cor. 8:4–13; Gal. 4:8–11, 5:6; Phil. 3:2–9). Peter soon came to see that if God can pronounce that certain foods that were formerly unclean are now acceptable, he can do the same thing with people. If it is now acceptable for Jews to eat the food of Gentiles, then the Gentiles themselves must now be considered as acceptable to God as well.

10:18 *who was known as Peter.* Jesus had renamed Simon "Peter," meaning "rock," because Jesus had foreseen that he would be the rock upon which the church would be built (Matt. 16:17–19).

10:19 *still thinking about the vision.* Peter was no doubt trying to determine what the vision meant in terms of actions he should or should not take. While he was seeking such direction, God sent him the answer in the form of the centurion's messengers.

10:20 *I have sent them.* The deity of the Spirit is shown here in that he speaks for God in the first person.

10:22 The men speak of Cornelius in a way to present him as favorably as possible to Peter. He is a God-fearer, respected by the Jews in his community. Since it would not be easy for a Roman to earn such Jewish respect, this was particularly impressive. What is more, an angel spoke to him about Peter, saying that he should listen to whatever Peter had to say to him. Thus prepared, Peter would have to be expectant that something especially important was about to occur.

10:23 While Jews would offer Gentiles hospitality, they typically would refuse to accept it from Gentiles lest they violate dietary laws. Assuming the messengers arrived in early afternoon (v. 9), it would have been too late in the day to start the 30-mile journey back to Caesarea.

Session 11
The Church in Antioch

Scripture   Acts 11:19–30

LAST WEEK

In last week's session we were reminded, along with Peter, that God's plan of salvation is open to everyone and what matters is the attitude of our heart, not the rules we follow. Today we see this new acceptance of Gentiles into the Christian faith spreading as the church grows in Antioch.

ICE-BREAKER   15 Min.
Connect with your Group

LEADER

Choose one, two or all three Ice-Breaker questions, depending on your group's needs.

The first Christians found themselves doing a lot of traveling and working in teams. Take turns sharing your own experiences with travel and teamwork.

1. What is the furthest you have traveled from home? What motivated you to go there?
    ❏ Business.
    ❏ Vacation.
    ❏ Mission.
    ❏ Other _____.

2. What has been your most memorable experience of working on a project with someone else? What helped you to work together as a team?

3. When have you been part of rallying to help a person or group in need? What role did you play? How did you feel about the help you were able to give?

BIBLE STUDY

30 Min.

READ SCRIPTURE AND DISCUSS

LEADER

Select a member of the group ahead of time to read the passage. Then discuss the Questions for Interaction, dividing into subgroups of four or five.

As our study of Acts continues, we see the church expanding to cities beyond Jerusalem and reaching out not just to Jews, but to Greeks as well. Read Acts 11:19–30 and note the importance of teamwork and support that helped to make the disciples' ministry successful and fruitful.

The Church in Antioch

¹⁹ Now those who had been scattered by the persecution in connection with Stephen traveled as far as Phoenicia, Cyprus and Antioch, telling the message only to Jews. ²⁰Some of them, however, men from Cyprus and Cyrene, went to Antioch and began to speak to Greeks also, telling them the good news about the Lord Jesus. ²¹The Lord's hand was with them, and a great number of people believed and turned to the Lord.

²²News of this reached the ears of the church at Jerusalem, and they sent Barnabas to Antioch. ²³When he arrived and saw the evidence of the grace of God, he was glad and encouraged them all to remain true to the Lord with all their hearts. ²⁴He was a good man, full of the Holy Spirit and faith, and a great number of people were brought to the Lord.

²⁵Then Barnabas went to Tarsus to look for Saul, ²⁶and when he found him, he brought him to Antioch. So for a whole year Barnabas and Saul met with the church and taught great numbers of people. The disciples were called Christians first at Antioch.

²⁷During this time some prophets came down from Jerusalem to Antioch. ²⁸One of them, named Agabus, stood up and through the Spirit predicted that a severe famine would spread over the entire Roman world. (This happened during the reign of Claudius.) ²⁹The disciples, each according to his ability, decided to provide help for the brothers living in Judea. ³⁰This they did, sending their gift to the elders by Barnabas and Saul.

Acts 11:19–30

LEADER

Refer to the Summary and Study Notes at the end of this session as needed. If 30 minutes is not enough time to answer all of the questions in this section, conclude the Bible Study by answering question #7.

QUESTIONS FOR INTERACTION

1. When has life "given you lemons" and you have been able to "make lemonade"? How did God help you in this process?

2. What actual benefit of the persecution of Christians in Jerusalem do we learn about in this story (vv. 19–20)? Would the Gospel have spread so fast to outlying areas had there not been persecution in Jerusalem? Why or why not?

3. What do you think encouraged those disciples from Cyprus and Cyrene to start sharing the Gospel with Greeks in Antioch, instead of only to Jews?
   ❒ News of Peter's vision (Acts 10).
   ❒ Special insight from the Holy Spirit.
   ❒ Other _____.

4. Why did the church at Jerusalem send Barnabas to Antioch?
   ❒ To check up on the Christians work.
   ❒ To help them out.
   ❒ To make a fuller report on their successes.
   ❒ Other _____.

5. Who did Barnabas go searching for to help him? Where did he find him? When had they had previous contact with each other (see 9:23–27)?

6. What special mission project are Barnabas and Saul given involving the Christians of Judea?

7. What ministry has God laid on your heart right now? What kind of person do you need to search out, like Barnabas searched for Saul, to help you with this ministry?

 GOING DEEPER: *If your group has time and/or wants a challenge, go on to this question.*

8. Are there people today to whom, like Agabus, God gives gifts of being able to forecast the future? What should the church be doing to look into the future and prepare for it?

CARING TIME   15 Min.

APPLY THE LESSON AND PRAY FOR ONE ANOTHER

LEADER

Conclude the prayer time by asking God for guidance in determining the future mission and outreach of this group.

The first Christians understood the importance of supporting and encouraging one another. Take this time now to support and encourage one another through sharing and prayer.

1. How has God been at work in your life this past week?

2. What is the biggest obstacle you're facing in the ministry God has called you to? How can the group help?

3. If God granted you a vision of this coming week, what would you want to know?

NEXT WEEK

Today we were given a wonderful opportunity to consider how the early Christians went about starting a new church and ministry. We saw how important teamwork is and how we all need support and help in carrying out the tasks that God sets before us. Be a Barnabas to someone in the coming week, and encourage that person in his or her spiritual walk. Next week we will be reminded of the importance of supporting one another in prayer and the miracles that can result, like Peter's miraculous escape from prison.

NOTES ON ACTS 11:19–30

Summary: Not all of those who contributed to the spread of the church in Acts got the same amount of "press" for their work. The work of Paul is given the greatest part of the book of Acts, taking up most of chapters 13–28. But others did important work about which little is written. Traditionally, it is said that Thomas took the Gospel to India. Peter is said to have started the church in Rome. But because little is written of this work, there is much we really don't know. Here in the eleventh chapter of Acts we learn of some people who did important mission work that is not given much recognition. Verses 19–21 tell of some disciples who took the Gospel to Antioch, a principle city in Syria. The church in Antioch eventually became quite an influential one, vying for a while with the Christian influence of cities like Jerusalem and Rome. But we don't even really know the names of those who started the church there! They are simply "those who had been scattered by the persecution" (v. 19).

Barnabas gets a little more recognition. That is probably because he was part of the original mission team with Paul. But Barnabas may be one of the most under-appreciated of our early Christian missionaries. He is the one who searches Saul (Paul) out to begin mission work with him in Antioch, and in their early work together his name is listed first, indicating that he was considered to be the most influential one (11:26; 13:2,7). He shared in Paul's first missionary journey, and when they broke up over the disagreement about John Mark, he himself headed a separate mission team that went to Cyprus. Nothing is recorded of his work there.

The example of people in this chapter is an important one for Christians. These disciples did significant work for the kingdom of God, but without getting much human credit. That is the experience of many down through time who have made great sacrifices, but who have done it for an eternal, rather than an earthly, reward (Matt. 6:4).

In this chapter we also see that persecution affected the Christian faith in positive ways, as well as negative. Nobody wants to wish persecution on fellow Christians (or fellow human beings, for that matter). But it did result in Christians who were more dedicated to their faith. It also forced believers to go out of their "comfort zone" to other parts of the world to share the Gospel. When the Romans leveled Jerusalem to the ground in A.D. 70, this was even more the case.

11:19 Since there were Jewish communities throughout the Roman Empire, it is not at all unusual that the Jewish believers would have spread throughout such a large area. **Phoenicia.** Modern Lebanon. **Antioch.** Located about 300 miles north of Jerusalem, this was the Roman capital of the province of Syria. It was the third-largest city in the Roman Empire (after Rome and Alexandria), with a population estimated at 750,000, including a Jewish community of 25,000. An early tradition teaches that Antioch was Luke's home.

11:20–21 These disciples from Cyprus and Cyrene were Jews who lived away from Judea and were used to interact with Gentiles. This broader mission does not necessarily represent a conscious decision to challenge accepted practice, however. Gentile God-fearers (like Cornelius) who were attracted to the ethics and values of

Judaism while not accepting its customs regarding food, circumcision and Sabbath regulations, undoubtedly attended the synagogues in Antioch. It is probably with these Gentiles that the believers shared the Gospel.

11:22 *they sent Barnabas.* Barnabas' function here is essentially the same as that performed by Peter and John after Philip's mission to Samaria (8:14–17). He was there at least in part to validate the ministry being done.

11:23 Barnabas did not require the Gentile converts to submit to Jewish traditions, but only encouraged them to maintain a heartfelt loyalty to Jesus as Lord. This is the essence of Christian discipleship.

11:24 *He was a good man.* Barnabas is first heard of in Acts 4:36–37 as one who sold a field and brought the money to the apostles' feet. He is there said to have been a Levite, and it is noted that his name meant "Son of Encouragement." He indeed was an encourager, as he encouraged the disciples to take a chance on Saul after Saul's conversion (9:26–27), and he encouraged Paul to take a chance on John Mark after John Mark's desertion on a missionary journey (15:36–41). The manner in which he is eulogized here ("he *was* a good man") would seem to indicate that he had died by the time of this writing.

11:26 *The disciples were called Christians.* By the time of Luke's writing, this Latin term was a widespread name for the believers. Previously, such believers referred to themselves as followers of the Way (9:2). As the Herodians were people loyal to Herod, so this name points out that the believers professed loyalty to Christ. Since the only other places in the New Testament where this term is used are situations of ridicule and persecution (26:28; 1 Peter 4:16), it may have been originally a name used to mock the believers.

11:27 *some prophets.* The Christian prophets were people who, through the inspiration of the Holy Spirit, spoke the message of Jesus to the contemporary situation facing the church, warning it of dangers and comforting it in trial (21:9–10; 1 Cor. 12:28; 14:1–5).

11:28 There was no single widespread famine during Claudius' reign (A.D. 41–54), but there were at least five localized famines during this period, including one that affected Judea around A.D. 46.

11:30 Whether Galatians 2:1–10 refers to this visit or the one Paul makes in Acts 15 is debated. Luke's point is to show the care of the church for its members and the emerging role of Paul as a recognized leader. There is probably a two to three year interval between the prophecy (v. 28) and the actual delivery of the gift.

SESSION 12
THE CHURCH PRAYS FOR PETER

SCRIPTURE ACTS 12:1–17

LAST WEEK

Last week we saw the importance of teamwork and an encouraging spirit when reaching out to others with the Gospel, as we observed Barnabas and other disciples minister to the Gentiles in Antioch. Today we will be inspired by the power of prayer and the miracle of Peter's escape from prison and certain death.

ICE-BREAKER   15 Min.
CONNECT WITH YOUR GROUP

LEADER

Choose one, two or all three of the Ice-Breaker questions, depending on your group's needs.

Life is full of surprises—both good and bad. Take turns sharing some of your unique experiences in life.

1. What is the closest you have come to spending time in jail? If you have spent time in jail, what was it like to get out?

2. When you were a child in grade school and you had a story to tell that was hard to believe, who would generally believe you when nobody else would?

3. When has something happened to you that was so good you didn't know if it was real or if you were dreaming?

BIBLE STUDY

READ SCRIPTURE AND DISCUSS

30 Min.

LEADER

Select a member of the group ahead of time to read the passage. Then discuss the Questions for Interaction, dividing into subgroups of four or five.

Can prayer really change things? In today's passage, Peter and his fellow Christians find that it indeed can! They are amazed when Peter is rescued from prison by an angel and escapes certain death at the hands of King Herod. Read Acts 12:1–17 and see how God answers the prayers of his people.

The Church Prays for Peter

12 It was about this time that King Herod arrested some who belonged to the church, intending to persecute them. ²He had James, the brother of John, put to death with the sword. ³When he saw that this pleased the Jews, he proceeded to seize Peter also. This happened during the Feast of Unleavened Bread. ⁴After arresting him, he put him in prison, handing him over to be guarded by four squads of four soldiers each. Herod intended to bring him out for public trial after the Passover.

⁵So Peter was kept in prison, but the church was earnestly praying to God for him.

⁶The night before Herod was to bring him to trial, Peter was sleeping between two soldiers, bound with two chains, and sentries stood guard at the entrance. ⁷Suddenly an angel of the Lord appeared and a light shone in the cell. He struck Peter on the side and woke him up. "Quick, get up!" he said, and the chains fell off Peter's wrists.

⁸Then the angel said to him, "Put on your clothes and sandals." And Peter did so. "Wrap your cloak around you and follow me," the angel told him. ⁹Peter followed him out of the prison, but he had no idea that what the angel was doing was really happening; he thought he was seeing a vision. ¹⁰They passed the first and second guards and came to the iron gate leading to the city. It opened for them by itself, and they went through it. When they had walked the length of one street, suddenly the angel left him.

¹¹Then Peter came to himself and said, "Now I know without a doubt that the Lord sent his angel and rescued me from Herod's clutches and from everything the Jewish people were anticipating."

¹²When this had dawned on him, he went to the house of Mary the mother of John, also called Mark, where many people had gathered and were praying. ¹³Peter knocked at the outer entrance, and a servant girl named Rhoda came to answer the door. ¹⁴When she recognized Peter's voice, she was so overjoyed she ran back without opening it and exclaimed, "Peter is at the door!"

15"You're out of your mind," they told her. When she kept insisting that it was so, they said, "It must be his angel."

16But Peter kept on knocking, and when they opened the door and saw him, they were astonished. 17Peter motioned with his hand for them to be quiet and described how the Lord had brought him out of prison. "Tell James and the brothers about this," he said, and then he left for another place.

Acts 12:1–17

QUESTIONS FOR INTERACTION

LEADER

Refer to the Summary and Study Notes at the conclusion of this session as needed. If 30 minutes is not enough time to answer all of the questions in this section, conclude the Bible Study by answering question #7.

1. Why was Herod persecuting the church?

2. Why was Herod waiting until after the Passover to deal with Peter?

3. Had you been Peter, which of the events of this story would you have found most surprising?

4. Where did Peter go after he was released from prison? Why was he received there in the way that he was?

5. Why do you think God delivered Peter from prison, but not James (v. 2)?

6. In your opinion, what is the most important effect this event had on the life of the church in Jerusalem?

7. When has God surprised you with the way he answered one of your prayers?

GOING DEEPER: *If your group has time and/or wants a challenge, go on to this question.*

8. Given that some people (like Peter) are "delivered from prison" after prayer, while some (like James) are not, how should the church pray? What encouragement can be given to the friends and loved ones of "James"?

CARING TIME   15 Min.

APPLY THE LESSON AND PRAY FOR ONE ANOTHER

LEADER

Following the Caring Time, discuss with your group how they would like to celebrate the last session next week. Also, discuss the possibility of splitting into two groups and continuing with another study (perhaps Book 2 of the study of Acts).

Realizing the power of prayer to change things, take some time now to pray for one another.

1. When have you prayed for something for a long period of time without getting an answer? What prayer requests do you have now that you are anxious for God to answer?

2. When has God answered one of your prayers recently? How did you respond?

3. Have each group member share on the question, "From what 'prison' do you need to be released right now?" Then pray for God to release each other from these "prisons."

NEXT WEEK

Today we were reminded of the importance of prayer and encouraged by the fact that God always answers prayer, even though it may not be in the way we expect him to! In the coming week, make a list of your prayer requests and record the way God answers each one in the future. Next week will be the last session in this first book on the study of Acts. We will be looking at an exciting story about the ministry of Paul and Barnabas, and how they persevered in spite of the obstacles of misunderstanding and hate.

NOTES ON ACTS 12:1-17

Summary: Prayer was an important part of the church of Acts. But as we see in this passage, even in that church, people didn't always understand its potential. What they learned in this incident can be an important lesson for the church today as well.

The story starts with some ominous actions by King Herod. Herod Agrippa I was popular with the Jews, and to further cultivate this popularity he resumed the persecution of the church, which had ceased upon Paul's conversion (9:31). James, the brother of John and one of the sons of Zebedee, was killed with the sword under this persecution. Also, Peter was arrested. They were a church under pressure, and in the midst of that pressure they turned to prayer.

Herod's intent was eventually to have Peter killed, as he had James. But he was waiting until "after the Passover," as such an execution during the Passover would have been seen as sacrilegious (Mark 14:2). He handed Peter over to "four squads of four soldiers each" (v. 4). However, even that wasn't sufficient to thwart the power of God! He sent an angel who delivered Peter from the prison. After his escape, Peter went to the home of Mary, the mother of John Mark. John Mark was the one who wrote the Gospel of Mark. The disciples had gathered there and were praying. What were they praying for? To answer that question, we only have to refer back to verse 5, "So Peter was kept in prison, but the church was earnestly praying to God for him." A maid named Rhoda, who was also part of the Christian community, greeted Peter. She was so stunned that she didn't even think to let Peter in! So with the possibility that the Sanhedrin had already sent guards out looking for him, she left Peter standing outside at the gate! She reported Peter's presence, which the disciples did not believe. Thus this event is similar to Christ's resurrection (Luke 24:5–11), where the disciples did not believe the report of the women that Christ had been raised. Luke, also the author of Acts, was sympathetic to women, and may have been chiding the male disciples for not taking the women in their midst seriously.

And so we see that the disciples were gathered praying for a divine intervention to save Peter from what happened to James. God heard their prayer and sent an angel to deliver Peter safely to them. But when he arrived, these praying disciples did not believe what had happened!

This story reminds us that while God does not always give us what we pray for (James, after all, was not delivered), we should still pray expecting God to answer our prayers with power and to his glory. That is what it means to pray with a faith that can "move mountains" (Matt. 17:20–21).

12:1 *King Herod.* This is Herod Agrippa I, the grandson of Herod the Great, who ruled when Jesus was born, and the nephew of Herod Antipas who governed Galilee during Jesus' ministry. Herod Agrippa I was popular with the Jews; some even wondered if he might be the Messiah who would free them from Rome. To further cultivate this popularity, he resumed the persecution of the church, which had ceased upon Paul's conversion (9:31). Since Herod died in A.D. 44, this story precedes the visit of Paul and Barnabas to Jerusalem (11:27–30).

12:7 *a light shone.* Similarities between this story and other escape stories circulating in the first century have led some commentators to assume that supernatural overtones were added to an account of how Peter was released with the help of a sympathetic insider. However, this fails to account for how the security measures used to imprison Peter could have been circumvented. Four soldiers on six-hour shifts constantly guarded Peter (vv. 4,6). Two soldiers were in the cell with Peter chained to their wrists, while the other two stood guard at the door. Such intense security measures may have been implemented precisely to prevent any such "unexplainable" release such as happened when the Sanhedrin had imprisoned him earlier (5:19–24). The description of the light, a common symbol of divine glory, underscores that this was a miraculous intervention of God.

12:8–10 In a trance-like state, Peter was led past the prison's guard and through the main gate of the prison.

12:11 *the Lord ... rescued me from Herod's clutches.* In Acts, there is no predictable pattern of how God will work. While Peter was released from prison, James, for whom the church undoubtedly prayed just as earnestly, was killed. Dorcas, a kindly but relatively insignificant woman (9:36–41), is raised from the dead while a bold, courageous man like Stephen is not. Even in this account, Peter, although so miraculously protected by God, decides he should go into hiding lest Herod catch him again (v. 17). The answer to why these things should be so is not given. The mystery is only known in the secret counsel of God who works all things according to his will. The call to the church is to be faithful and take responsible action whether or not God chooses to act in a miraculous way.

12:12 *Mary the mother of John, also called Mark.* This is the Mark who later wrote the Gospel bearing that name (12:25; 13:5).

12:13–17 In a humorous way, Luke recounts how Peter was left standing at the gate of the courtyard while the disciples refused to believe that he could possibly be there!

12:15 *It must be his angel.* It was believed that each person had a guardian angel who watched over that individual. Assuming that Peter was killed, the only solution the disciples could come up with was that Peter's angel had taken on Peter's form.

12:17 *James.* This is the half-brother of Jesus (Mark 6:3). James did not believe in Jesus as the Messiah during Jesus' ministry (John 7:5), but after the Resurrection Jesus appeared to him in a special way (1 Cor. 15:7), qualifying James to be an apostle. James became a leader in the Jerusalem church (15:13; 21:18; Gal. 2:9), and his piety and devotion to God gained the respect of the Jewish community in general. When executed by the Sadducean high priest in A.D. 61, his death was mourned by many Pharisaic Jews as well as Christians. *he left for another place.* While Peter recognized his release as an act of God, he did not believe that made him invulnerable to Herod's plots. Thus, he left Jerusalem for some time. Although Peter was in Jerusalem at the time of the council in Acts 15, nothing more is told of his story in Acts. Church tradition associates him with travels to Alexandria, Asia Minor, and finally Rome where he was crucified upside down by the Emperor Nero.

SESSION 13
PAUL AND BARNABAS IN LYSTRA

SCRIPTURE   ACTS 14:8–20

LAST WEEK

In last week's session we saw that prayer really can change things! Peter escaped prison and death when an angel rescued him, just as the disciples were gathered to pray for him. Today we will conclude our study of Acts by learning from Paul and Barnabas as they face misunderstanding and danger while spreading the good news of Jesus.

ICE-BREAKER   15 Min.
CONNECT WITH YOUR GROUP

LEADER

Begin this final session with a word of prayer and thanksgiving for this time together. Choose one or two Ice-Breaker questions to discuss.

We have probably all wondered what it would be like to be famous. Today's society treats celebrities almost as "gods." However, negative publicity can turn us against these celebrities just as fast. Take turns sharing your thoughts and feelings on "fame."

1. When you were in junior high, who were you most likely to think of as "gods"?
  ❏ Sports figures.
  ❏ Singers.
  ❏ Movie stars.
  ❏ Your parents.
  ❏ Other _____.

2. In junior high, who seemed to go out of their way to discredit you?

3. Finish this sentence: "The last time I felt I was really treated 'like a god' was when ..."

BIBLE STUDY
READ SCRIPTURE AND DISCUSS

30 Min.

LEADER

Select a member of the group ahead of time to read the passage. Then discuss the Questions for Interaction, dividing into subgroups of four or five.

People throughout the ages have worshiped the things and people that God created, rather than the Creator himself. In today's Scripture passage, we see this happen to the people of Lystra. They completely miss the message of salvation that Paul and Barnabas are sharing and start worshiping the messengers themselves. Read Acts 14:8–20 and note how Paul and Barnabas respond to this situation.

Paul and Barnabas in Lystra

⁸In Lystra there sat a man crippled in his feet, who was lame from birth and had never walked. ⁹He listened to Paul as he was speaking. Paul looked directly at him, saw that he had faith to be healed, ¹⁰and called out, "Stand up on your feet!" At that, the man jumped up and began to walk.

¹¹When the crowd saw what Paul had done, they shouted in the Lycaonian language, "The gods have come down to us in human form!" ¹²Barnabas they called Zeus, and Paul they called Hermes because he was the chief speaker. ¹³The priest of Zeus, whose temple was just outside the city, brought bulls and wreaths to the city gates because he and the crowd wanted to offer sacrifices to them.

¹⁴But when the apostles Barnabas and Paul heard of this, they tore their clothes and rushed out into the crowd, shouting: ¹⁵"Men, why are you doing this? We too are only men, human like you. We are bringing you good news, telling you to turn from these worthless things to the living God, who made heaven and earth and sea and everything in them. ¹⁶In the past, he let all nations go their own way. ¹⁷Yet he has not left himself without testimony: He has shown kindness by giving you rain from heaven and crops in their seasons; he provides you with plenty of food and fills your hearts with joy." ¹⁸Even with these words, they had difficulty keeping the crowd from sacrificing to them.

¹⁹Then some Jews came from Antioch and Iconium and won the crowd over. They stoned Paul and dragged him outside the city, thinking he was dead. ²⁰But after the disciples had gathered around him, he got up and went back into the city. The next day he and Barnabas left for Derbe.

Acts 14:8–20

LEADER

Refer to the Summary and Study Notes at the end of this session as needed. If 30 minutes is not enough time to answer all of the questions in this section, conclude the Bible Study by answering question #7.

QUESTIONS FOR INTERACTION

1. In general, do you feel like people treat you better than you deserve, as the Lycaonians did with Paul and Barnabas at first; or worse than you deserve, as they treated Paul and Barnabas after the Jewish instigators came along?

2. What language were the people shouting in? How do you suppose that affected the understanding of Paul and Barnabas as to what was going on at first?

3. What upset Paul and Barnabas so much when they realized the crowd was getting ready to offer sacrifices to them?

4. How did Paul and Barnabas express their feelings once they realized that they were being thought of as gods (v. 14)?

5. After they realize that they are being thought of as gods, what are the main points of the message that Paul and Barnabas make to the crowd (vv. 15–17)?

6. Why was the crowd that had previously proclaimed Paul and Barnabas as gods, so quickly persuaded to stone them?

7. Who do you even now have a tendency to treat as more than just another human being?
❐ Your spouse.
❐ Your parents.
❐ A pastor or other spiritual leader.
❐ The president.
❐ Other _____.

What change of attitude does this story call you to have concerning that person?

GOING DEEPER: *If your group has time and/or wants a challenge, go on to this question.*

8. Why is it that we have this tendency to turn our leaders into "gods"? What need do you think this fulfills? What should church leaders do to guard against this tendency?

CARING TIME   15 Min.
APPLY THE LESSON AND PRAY FOR ONE ANOTHER

LEADER

Conclude this final Caring Time by praying for each group member and asking for God's blessing in any plans to start a new group and/or continue to study together.

In today's passage, we saw the disciples gather around Paul after he was stoned and give him the strength to go on (v. 20). Gather around each other now in this prayer time and give each other the strength and support to go out and share Christ with others.

1. What have you gained from this study of Acts (chapters 1–14)? How can you help your church to carry out the Great Commission and spread the Gospel to your community?

2. Take time to share, "What has God done recently that has 'filled your heart with joy' (v. 17)?" Thank God for these things in prayer.

3. What will you remember most about this group? How would you like the group to continue praying for you?

WHAT'S NEXT?

Today we saw how sharing the Good News can lead to difficult and even dangerous circumstances. We also saw how much we need each other in order to carry on and fulfill the ministry that God has planned for each and every one of us. If your group has decided to continue with studying Book 2 of Acts, the next session will look at the early church beginning to debate the issue of works vs. faith. This is a topic that remains an issue to this very day!

NOTES ON ACTS 14:8–20

Summary: Paul and his companions relied on the power of God to do great things, and as a result, great things happened. But this, in turn, meant that some people mistook the power of God working through them for them actually being gods. This is what occurred in Lystra on Paul's first missionary journey. Lystra was the hometown of Timothy (16:1–2). There were already two local legends that told of times when Zeus and Hermes had come down in human likeness: (1) Lycaon entertained these gods by feasting them on human flesh, and was turned into a wolf for doing so; (2) on the second occasion, Baucis and Philemon, an elderly couple, were the only people who welcomed the gods, and were rewarded by being allowed to die at the same time so neither would have to mourn the other. This is important background information that helps us understand why the people here were so quick to declare Paul and Barnabas to be gods.

What happened at this place? Paul healed a man who had been lame since birth. When this healing happened the people got excited and started speaking in their native tongue, Lycaonian, rather than in the Greek that Paul was speaking. Because of this Paul and the others probably didn't understand at first what they were saying. Their initial statement was, "The gods have come down to us in human form!" (v. 11). They believed that their legends were true and were now happening again. The reason that Paul and Barnabas didn't react negatively right away to being idolized in such a way was that they didn't understand Lycaonian, the language in which the people were saying these things.

In verse 13 we find that people came from the temple of Zeus outside the city and wanted to offer sacrifice, so all of this must have taken some time. Verse 14 tells us that when Paul and Barnabas heard of it they tore their clothes. This was a sign of repentance and mourning. They were shocked that people were treating them as gods, and didn't want there to be any thought that they were encouraging such a practice. They were there to teach about the true God, and they wanted no part of idolatry, especially if THEY were being made into the idols! Accepting the status of a god was the worst kind of blasphemy, a crime that would have warranted the death sentence in Jewish culture, which interestingly enough is the penalty that the instigators from Antioch and Iconium later seek to impose.

Perhaps the most fascinating aspect of what happens here is that after Paul and Barnabas refuse to be treated as gods, the crowd is turned all the way around and convinced to treat them as criminals, going so far as to stone Paul! This illustrates the dangers involved when a crowd wants to use a person for their own ends and are frustrated. It is reminiscent of how the Palm Sunday crowd was frustrated when Jesus did not take on Rome militarily, and then similarly turned and called for his death.

14:8 The small Jewish community in Lystra (16:1–3) apparently did not have a synagogue. Adopting a new strategy that brought the Gospel directly to the Gentiles, Paul probably preached in the Greek forum, the site of the local market place and gathering place for public discussion.

14:9 *saw that he had faith to be healed.* How did he see this? Did he show it in a positive demeanor, in how he treated the people around him, or in the statements of faith he was making? Perhaps all of the above! In any case, we consistently see in Scripture that faith is a necessary element in healing (see for instance Matt.9:20–22, 27–31).

14:11 An ancient legend said that Jupiter and Mercury (the Latin counterparts to Zeus and Hermes) appeared to a couple in a nearby area. As a result, the local people made pilgrimages to this site and the worship to these gods flourished in the region through the third century A.D.

14:12 *Hermes ... the chief speaker.* Zeus was the chief god among the Greek deities, while Hermes was the herald of the gods. The fact that Paul was identified with Hermes shows that he was the leading figure in this missionary enterprise.

14:14 *they tore their clothes.* In the ancient world, this was a universally recognized sign of horror and grief. By so doing, the missionaries demonstrate the intensity of their opposition to what the people were supposedly doing in their honor.

14:15–17 Paul declares he and Barnabas are in no way divine, but only human messengers bringing a message from the one true, living God. He goes on to describe God as the Creator, the Sovereign over history, and the One who demonstrates his goodness by providing people with food and joy in life. It is this God alone who is to be worshiped and honored.

14:19–20 Although there was not a sufficient Jewish community in Lystra to cause any opposition, some traditional Jewish zealots who had traveled from Antioch (over 150 miles away) and Iconium reflected Paul's former zeal in opposing the Gospel by traveling to Lystra to stir up the people against him.

14:20 *he got up.* While some consider this a miracle of resurrection, Luke gives no indication that this was so. Paul was badly beaten and bruised, but able to travel on to Derbe. Paul refers to this incident in 2 Corinthians 11:25 with no mention of any miraculous resurrection or recovery.

Personal Notes

Personal Notes

Personal Notes

Personal Notes

Personal Notes

Personal Notes